# Indian Christian Women Pioneers and Leaders Revealed

**Christian Heritage Rediscovered**

The Series, as the name suggests, is meant to focus on Christian Faith & Living vis-à-vis topics like Literature & Poetry, Indigenous Philosophizing, Ethical response towards Agriculture, Health & Healing, Science & Technology, Eco-feminist Theology, Sociological approach towards Human Rights, Law & Politics, Arts, History of Ideas, Ancient Civilizations, Cultural Contiguity, Religious Cosmologies & Mysticism, Footsteps of famous Theologians, World Peace & Harmony, Global Capitalism, Network Marketing, Cybertheology, Population & Demographics, Epigraphic Studies, Contextualized Education, and many others. We welcome a Mss. on any topic/s mentioned, whether they are original works, scholarly monographs, collections of conference papers, revised dissertations, or translations of historical documents. Through the Series we, the Publishers, are striving to put forward published works that may help Institutions, Academic Bodies, Researchers, Scholars and the World at large in furthering their respective knowledge and understanding on the concerned subject. We welcome your comments on our efforts and further suggestions on how we can foster the upcoming thought provoking theologically grounded books.

*Christian Heritage Rediscovered - 44*

# Indian Christian Women Pioneers and Leaders Revealed

## An Exploration of Overlooked Women Voices in Socio-Cultural & Religious Framework

**Clara Mathew Shiju**

CWI
Christian World Imprints(TM)

First Published in 2017 by

**Christian World Imprints**™
*Christian Publishing & Books from India*
H-12 Bali Nagar, **New Delhi-110015**
info@christianworldimprints.com
www.ChristianWorldImprints.com
Phone: +91 11 25465925

ISBN 13: 978-93-5148-231-4 ISBN 10: 93-5148-231-6

**Cataloging in Publication Data--DK**
Courtesy: D.K. Agencies (P) Ltd. <docinfo@dkagencies.com>

**Mathew Shiju, Clara,** 1973- **author.**
Indian Christian women pioneers and leaders revealed : an exploration of overlooked women voices in socio-cultural & religious framework / Clara Mathew Shiju.
pages cm. -- (Christian heritage rediscovered ; 44)
Originally presented as the author's thesis (D.Min.--Senate of Serampore College) under the title: 'A wholistic leadership development programme for women in the Assemblies of God in Kannur District, Kerala'.
Includes bibliographical references.
ISBN 9351482316
ISBN 9789351482314

1. Christian leadership--India--Cannanore (District) 2. Christian leadership--Assemblies of God. 3. Women in church work--India--Cannanore (District) 4. Women in church work--Assemblies of God. 5. Pentecostalism--India--Kerala--History. I. Title. II. Series: Christian heritage rediscovered ; 44.

LCC BV676.M38 2017 | DDC 262.1082095483 23



Printed in India.

**Dedicated**

to my parents,

husband Shiju Mathew

and

children Freny and Reuel

# Contents

# Foreword

I am delighted to introduce the book entitled *Indian Christian Women Pioneers and Leaders Revealed* written by Clara Shiju Mathew as this work is a genuine exploration of overlooked women voices in a particular socio-cultural and religious framework. This is an upgraded version of her D. Min thesis entitled "A Wholistic Leadership Development Programme for Women in the Assemblies of God in Kannur District, Kerala". I encourage this publication mainly because of its originality and strong data presented in the work. Her suggestions are indeed helpful in promoting a possible ecclesiology in our context. The main suggestions are:

1. Theological trainings in an intentional manner (not only giving training, but also engaging them in church related activities, including leadership).
2. Adequate leadership roles such as Sunday school superintendent, women fellowship office bearers, part of decision making bodies, pastors and Superintendents etc.
3. Women empowerment/awareness programmes.
4. Exposure programmes.

Since this work was based on a systematic field study, it may inspire the people who are working at the grass-root level namely missionaries, evangelists and women workers. Dr. Clara has analyzed the data scientifically with the help of an appropriate methodology with a clear theological focus. Though she worked within the traditional ecclesial and theological framework, she could move beyond the myopic identities of gender. More importantly her study seems to be an eye opener in terms of understanding the ministry of the church with the help of newly coined terminologies and phrases.

Finally, I should mention that both Dr. Shiju Mathew and Clara Shiju Mathew have been responsible theological educators in our context by offering meaningful ministry. This study is a search for an ideal space for ministry of women in the church and society. May God enable Clara Shiju Mathew to publish more books in the coming years. I enthusiastically present this book.

**C. I. David Joy**
Professor, NT
United Theological College, Bangalore

# Acknowledgements

At the very beginning I would like to thank Sovereign God for His grace and blessings upon my life. I am very much grateful to my mentor Dr. Simon Samuel for his guidance throughout my research. I would like to express my heart-felt gratitude to Dr. Wati Longchar, Dr. M.T. Cherian, Dr. David Joy, Dr. James Venmani, Pastor Selvaraj and many others who contributed immensely during my theological journey. I express gratitude and sincere thanks to faculty and staff of United Theological College, Bangalore; Bethel Bible College, Punalur; Southern Asia Bible College, Bangalore; and New Theological College, Dehradun for helping me to have library resources.

I express my thanks to SCEPTRE for providing me scholarship during my Doctor in Ministry research period. I am indebted to our founders Uncle George & Auntie Leela and Managing Director Rev. George C Kuruvilla for their valuable prayer and blessings in my life.

I am so grateful to my parents and siblings for imparting Christian values in my life. My special thanks to my husband Dr. Shiju Mathew for being with me throughout my research period and taking care of home and children when I was away for research purpose.

# Abstract

Women consist of an equal or larger grouping within the Assemblies of God in the Kannur district in Kerala, India. Yet they do not have a proper and proportional level of involvement in ministry and in leadership roles or positions in the church. This I believe is due to a patriarchal and kyriarchal mindset in the reading of the Bible and also due to an inadequate development and promotional programs for women to enter into and rise up in the Christian ministry in the AG church. Therefore, this work attempts to promote and evolve a wholistic leadership development programme for women to enter into Christian ministry in the AG Church in general and Kannur district in particular.

The Pentecostal and Charismatic movements made remarkable in roads and as a result impacted Indian Christian circles for the last hundred years or so. In the rise and development of these movements, women too played significant parts. But their roles, functions and contributions are not recorded or recognized sufficiently in the historical records and writings of the churches or these movements. Their roles and positions are mostly seen as pastors' wives or as wandering prayer charismatics/evangelists, Sunday school teachers or leaders of the women wing of the church.

During the research, I found out that in the growth of the AG church, women too played crucial roles. Where men had no access, it was women who went in and shared the good news of Jesus. In spite of all their contributions, they are placed in the periphery both within the Church in general and in the AG church in particular. History seems silent about their roles and contributions.

The pertinent questions before us therefore are: Why the native Christian women preachers, evangelists, prayer enthusiasts and educators did not enter in the AG history? Why the AG church failed to develop women leaders? Why the door is now almost shut before many Christian women from entering into leading roles in the AG churches? What are some of the ways which can lead to women's wholistic leadership development programme for AG church in Kannur District?

A few historians from the Pentecostal and Charismatic churches from India have now written on the origin and growth of the AG church in India. Prominent among them are A. C. George and V. V. Thomas. As far as I am aware the role of women Christian preachers and teachers in Kannur area are not documented and studied by them. So, this project is an attempt to highlight this neglect and also to develop a programme for the wholistic ministry development for women in the AG church specially in the Kannur district.

## Methodology and Structure

## Methodology

The methodology for the research is mainly empirical data collection and interviews. Empirical research is done to find the role of Christian women in the growth of AG churches in Kannur district in Kerala. Besides this, a few interviews of the elderly believers in my area in Kannur where the AG churches are growing in recent years are taken.

The empirical data collection is then analyzed and critically reflected upon to see what the 'take aways' are so that an effective and relevant development program can be proposed for women to enter into and rise up in ministry in the AG church.

Library materials are also referred for examining the involvement of women in witnessing Christ in early Christianity, as well as in the later history of the Church including the Pentecostal and Charismatic churches.

For the history section, I used a revisionist feminist historiographal approach to critique andro-centric Indian historiography and reclaim an avenue for feminist and womanist historiography.

## Structure

Apart from introduction and conclusion, the whole work is divided into four chapters.

The first chapter is on the origin and growth of Pentecostal and Charismatic Movements in Kerala. In this chapter, I brought out the origin of Christianity in India, growth of Christianity from first century through 21$^{st}$ century and the beginning of Charismatic and Pentecostal, development and growth of Pentecostalism in Kerala, and role of both foreign and native missionaries.

The second chapter focuses on the role of women leaders in the origin and growth of the Pentecostal and Charismatic movements in Kerala. In this chapter the need and importance of a revisionist feminist historiography is spelled out to point out the problems of history written by male stream historians and reconstruct history by giving space and voice to women. This chapter also deals with the role of women leaders in the Pentecostal churches and their contributions.

The third chapter is on the status and role of women in the present day AG churches in general and in Kannur district in particular. This chapter, starts with a brief history of the AG church in Kerala. Other areas addressed in this chapter are status and role of women in the formation of AG church in Kerala, the role and ministry of native women missionaries in AG in Kerala, a brief history of Christianity in Kannur, and the contributions of women missionaries in the growth and development of AG church in Kannur.

The fourth chapter is on proposals for leadership development programme for women in AG church in Kannur district. Here, I brought out the demographic details of the respondents from whom I collected empirical data, survey on 'leadership role of women in the AG church in Kannur, challenges and prospects, critical study of women's leadership role in the AG in Kannur district', proposals for empowering women leadership in the church and the need for women leadership development programme

## Evaluation and steps to be taken for promoting women leaders in AG Church

Though women constitute the major constituency in the AG church and are actively involved in all church related activities, but unfortunately their contributions are taken lightly and often neglected by the male historians. The researcher strongly feels that some bold initiative is needed to address this crucial issue. Some of the viable alternatives to address this issue are by providing reasonable space to women both within and outside the church, formulating leadership development programme for women and implanting it with a broader mindset.

Some of the steps need to be taken for developing women leadership are:

1. Theological trainings in an intentional manner (not only giving training, but also engaging them in church related activities, including leadership).
2. Adequate leadership roles such as Sunday school superintendent, women fellowship office bearers, part of decision making bodies, pastors and Superintendents etc.
3. Women empowerment/awareness programmes.
4. Exposure programmes.

If these steps are implemented properly, it will enhance the growth of the AG Church.

# Introduction

## 1.1. Statement of the Problem

Women consist of an equal or a larger grouping within the Assemblies of God (henceforth AG Church) in Kannur district in Kerala, India. Yet, they do not have a proper and proportional level of involvement in ministry and in leadership roles or positions in the church. This I believe is due to a patriarchal and kyriarchal mindset in the reading of the Bible and also due to an inadequate development and promotional programs for women to enter into and rise up in the Christian ministry in the AG church.

Therefore, this book attempts to promote and evolve a wholistic leadership development programme for women to enter into Christian ministry in the AG church in general and Kannur district in particular.

## 1.2. Elaboration of the Problem

The Pentecostal and Charismatic movements have made remarkable in roads and as a result impacted Indian Christian circles for the last hundred years or so. In the rise and development of these movements, women too played significant parts. But their roles, functions and contributions are not recorded or recognized sufficiently in the historical records and writings of the churches or these movements. Their roles and positions are mostly seen as pastors' wives, wandering prayer charismatics/evangelists, Sunday school teachers or leaders of the women wing of the church.

For preliminary investigation, I had extensive conversations with my pastor and a few elderly women of the AG church in Kannur. During my conversations, I found out that in the growth of the AG church, women too played crucial roles. Where men had no access, it was women who went in and shared the good news of Jesus. In spite of all their contributions, they are placed in the periphery both within the church in general and in the AG church in particular. History seems silent about their roles and contributions.

The pertinent questions before us therefore are: Why the native Christian women preachers, evangelists, prayer enthusiasts and educators did not enter in the AG church history? Why the AG church failed to develop women leaders? Why the door is now almost shut before many Christian women from entering into leading roles in the AG churches? What are some of the ways which can lead to women's wholistic leadership development programme for AG church in Kannur District?

## 1.3. Importance of the Problem

I think that this topic is important because women occupy more than half the space in the Christian churches in general and in the Pentecostal and Charismatic churches in particular. But, the roles of women in the podium and in other positions of leadership in the present day churches are almost nil. I strongly feel that this research work will provoke many and help leaders to develop a program. I do suggest a few ways and means which will contribute towards a wholistic leadership development programme for women in the AG church in Kannur district.

## 1.4. Previous Research

The involvement of Christian women in witnessing Christ even as leaders in the early Christian community is investigated quite thoroughly by a few women scholars like Elizabeth Schüssler Fiorenza, Kwok-Pui-Lan, Christina Manohar, and others. I would like to use their methods, writings and leads as a foundation, launch pad and supporting tool to prepare a programme for wholistic leadership development programme for women in the AG church in Kannur district[1].

A few historians from the Pentecostal and Charismatic churches from India have now written on the origin and growth of the AG church in India. Prominent among them are A. C. George, Saju and V. V. Thomas. As far as, I am aware the role of women Christian preachers and teachers in Kannur area are not documented and studied by them. So, this project is an attempt to highlight this neglect and also to develop a programme for the wholistic ministry development for women in the AG church specially in the Kannur district.

## 1.5. Methodology and Structure

### Methodology

The methodology for the research will be empirical data collection and interviews.

Empirical research will be done to find the role of Christian women in the growth of AG churches in Kannur district in Kerala. I would also do a few interviews of elderly believers in my area in Kannur where the AG churches are growing in recent years.

Criteria for selecting interviews for empirical survey:
Duration of the person's membership in the church
Role/roles of the person in the church
Status of the person
Economic
Social
Gender
Age
Educational Qualification
Ethnic/Cultural Background

The empirical data collection will then be analyzed and critically reflected upon to see what the 'take aways' are so that an effective and

1 The reason for choosing AG Church in Kannur district is because I hail from Kannur.

relevant development program can be proposed for women to enter into and rise up in ministry in the AG church.

Library materials will be referred for examining the involvement of women in witnessing Christ in early Christianity, as well as in the later history of the churches including the Pentecostal and Charismatic churches.

For the history section, I used a revisionist feminist historiographal approach to critique andro-centric Indian historiography and reclaim an avenue for feminist and womanist historiography.

## Structure

Apart from introduction and conclusion, the whole work is divided into four chapters.

The first chapter is on the origin and growth of Pentecostal and Charismatic Movements in Kerala.

The second chapter focuses on the role of women leaders in the origin and growth of the Pentecostal and Charismatic movement in Kerala

The third chapter is on the status and role of women in the present day AG churches in general and in Kannur district in particular.

The fourth chapter is on proposals for leadership development programme for Women in AG church in Kannur District.

## 1.6. Scope and Limitation

The scope of this research is limited to explore the place and roles of women in Pentecostal church in India and in Kerala in general and in Kannur District. It proposes a development programme for their wholistic leadership ministry in the AG church in Kannur district.

I will limit my empirical research to 25-30 larger and smaller churches throughout Kannur District.

Chapter 1

# Origin and Growth of the Pentecostal and Charismatic Movements in Kerala

## Introduction

In this chapter I would like to explore (i) the origin and growth of Christianity in India, (ii) the beginning of Charismatic and Pentecostal movements in the West and in India, and (iii) the role of men and women behind the growth and development of Pentecostalism in India. The main focus of this chapter will be on the origin and growth of Pentecostal and Charismatic movements in Kerala.

## 1.1. A Brief Sketch of the Origin and Growth of Christianity in India

### 1.1.1. The Historical Background of Christianity in India

According to the Eastern and Western traditions, Christianity was brought in India in the first century by St. Thomas, one of the twelve Apostles of Jesus Christ.[2] He was one of those chosen by Jesus as His

---

2 C. B. Firth, *An Introduction to Indian Church History,* (Serampore: The Indian Theological Library, 1961), 2, A. M. Mundadan, *History of Christianity in India*, Vol. 1, (Bangalore: CHAI, 1989), 3.

apostle. The Syrian Christian tradition and many of the early Christian writers and historians tells us that the foundation of Christianity in India was laid by St. Thomas in 52 A.D.[3] As a member of the twelve disciples, he was also a participant of the Jerusalem Pentecost (Acts 2). Being witnessed and practised the Pentecost experience, he in all possibility presented such experiences in his Christian practice in India too.[4] His ministry too was probably similar to that of Peter and Paul in the early days about which we read in Acts of the Apostles. A glimpse of his ministry can be gleaned from the *Acts of the Thomas* even though this book is seen as an Apocryphal Gospel.

### *1.1.1.1. Arrival of St. Thomas in India*

After the Jerusalem Pentecost and after being filled with the Holy Spirit the followers of Jesus devoted their ministry in the Mediterranean region (Acts of the Apostles chaps 8, 11, 13). In order to choose the location of ministry it is probable that lots were cast (c.f. Acts 1). The lot to go to India fell on Apostle Thomas. Tradition says that at first he rejected it but later God appeared to him in a vision and as a result came to North West part of India.[5] Thomas later on came by sea too, and he landed at Cranganore (Kerala) where he preached the gospel, performed miracles and converted high caste Hindu families.[6] He established a few churches.[7] Then he visited the Coromandel Coast (Madras region) sharing the gospel and many were converted. He crossed over to China and later returned to India and organized the Christians of Malabar under leaders from the leading members he had converted. He most definitely practiced and presented the same Christianity which the other Apostles in the first Christian centuries practised. In the Coromondel coast he suffered martyrdom near the

3 A. M. Mundadan, *History of Christianity in India.*

4 Simon Samuel, "The Charismatic and Pentecostal Movements and their Commitments to the Social Demands of the Gospel," *Doon Theological Journal,* 9.2 (2012): 222.

5 *Acts of the Thomas* cited in C. B. Firth, *An Introduction to Indian Church History,* (Serampore: The Indian Theological Library, 1961), 9.

6 This is according to the Eastern tradition alive in stories even today in Kerala.

7 There are debates on this matter. Tradition says that he founded seven and a half Church.

little mount (close to Madras now known as Chennai). His body was brought to the town of Mylapore and was buried in a holy shrine. Even today the Christians from Malabar, west Asia, and even from China used to come on pilgrimage to Mylapore and venerate the tomb.[8]

Even though, the St. Thomas tradition is so strong among the Thomas Christians in Kerala, its historicity cannot be proved because of the absence of hard historical evidences. But it is a living tradition for the Syrian Christians. Other than this living tradition there are historical evidences[9] to prove that Christianity existed in India from the fourth century A.D. For instance, there is evidence that the church in India was represented by John, "Bishop of Persia and Great India" at the Nicean Council held in 325 A.D. and that this bishop was one of the signatories in the "Acts of the Council of Nicea". Other than these evidences there are also archaeological evidences to support this view, such as, trade between India and the Roman Empire in the first century.[10] Based on all these evidences we can conclude that Christianity in India is as old as Christianity itself.[11]

## 1.2. The Origin of Pentecostal and Charismatic Movements

The origin of Pentecostal and Charismatic movements traces their beginning from the earliest phase from Apostle Thomas in India in AD 52 itself. They were an outcome of the spiritual experiences and practices of the first century believers of the early church.[12] In other words, Pentecostalism is that segment of Christianity which believes that there is a unique aspect of the Spirit's manifestation, namely baptism in the Spirit and the initial external evidence of speaking

8 A. M. Mundadan, *History of Christianity in India*, 29.

9 Copper plate inscriptions in Kottayam Seminary and Mar Thoma Headquarters.

10 Recent archaeological evidences at Cranganore show numerous numismatic evidences of trade between Romans and the Kerala Coast people.

11 A. C. George, "Pentecostal Beginnings in Travancore, South India", *AJPS* 4/2 (2001): 216.

12 Simon Samuel, "The Charismatic and Pentecostal Movements and their Commitments to the Social Demands of the Gospel," 214.

in tongues. Pentecostalism believes that this baptism in the Spirit is setting standard for every Christian believer. Pentecostalism also believe that the New Testament record of the event of Pentecost is not merely a "record of what happened in one generation, but a blue print and a type of what should happen in every generation until Jesus returns again."[13]

The Pentecostal movement is generally understood in terms of its characteristic expression such as the *glossolalia* (speaking in tongues). According to Dayton, speaking in tongues is evident only to those who are members of the "Pentecostal" churches, but the practice of "glossolalia is a common religious phenomenon."[14]

Those who claim themselves as "Pentecostals" relate their name and identity to the first followers of Jesus Christ who were filled with the promised Holy Spirit on the day of Pentecost (Act. 2). They believe that the manifestations of the Spirit with manifest evidence of speaking in tongues, prophecy and other spiritual gifts are available to all those who believe in Jesus Christ even today.[15]

It is evident from the New Testament that the first followers of Jesus Christ (both men and women) represented a small group drawn from the Jews and Gentiles. After the resurrection of Jesus Christ, they were filled with Holy Spirit in Jerusalem (Acts 2), Samaria (Acts 8), and among the Gentiles in Palestine, and in far distance place in Ephesus (Acts 19), in fulfilment of the promise of the risen Lord Jesus Christ. Many of those who experienced the Holy Spirit baptism were clearly women too and they actively participated and propagated the Gospel in the early church. This is seen in one of the Apocryphal Acts called *Acts of Paul and Techla.*

Elizabeth Fiorenza observes that the first witnesses of Jesus Christ were both men and women. But quite often the importance

---

13 V. V. Thomas, "Contribution of Ziegenbalg and William Carrey to India: Challenges to Mission of the Church in India Today: A Pentecostal Perspective," an unpublished paper presented at the seminar on 7th Feb 2006, 1.

14 Donald W. Dayton, *Theological Roots of Pentecostalism*, (Peabody: Hendrickson Publishers, 1987), 15.

15 Harvey Cox, *Fire from Heaven: The Rise of Pentecostal Spirituality and the Reshaping of Religion in the Twenty-First Century*, (Cambridge: Da Capo Press, 1995), 3.

of women and their leading roles in the early Christian beginnings are shunned due to the 'andro-centric historiography.' From the book of Acts of the Apostles and the Epistles it is clear that the early church was a movement of both men and women, e.g., Mary, Rhoda, Tabitha, Pricilla, Lydia, Euodia, Syntyche, Damarius, Phoebe, Junia, Tryphane, Tryphose, etc., had leading roles in the life and ministry of the early church. Some of these women were pastors (*prostasis*) who stand before others to lead them.[16] There was and is no distinction of gender in receiving anointing from the Holy Spirit. Paul's letters give ample evidences that women were active partners in the ministry and worship (Rom 16). Among them there were apostles, pastors and prophets. The daughters of Philip, the Evangelist were prophets. Church history too witnesses the different roles of women in ministry.[17]

According to Allan Anderson, 'The early church was a community of the Holy Spirit, and the freedom of expression and spontaneity of its worship may not have been very different from that of many Pentecostal and Charismatic churches today. Some of the characteristic features and ecstatic phenomena of Pentecostalism like prophecy, healing and speaking in tongues were common.'[18] This was experienced by both men and women and they led the church and ministry without any discrimination in the early church.

In the history of the post-apostolic times, Tertullian (the North African bishop, c, A.D. 155-220) was an advocate of the gifts of the Holy Spirit such as prophecy, visions and ecstasy. Tertullian also testified that *glossolalia* was found in the Montanist church which he had joined for some time. Irenaeus writes, "We have in the church many brethren who have the prophecy and speaking various kinds of tongues through the spirit."[19] Bishop Ignatius of Antioch speaks of an ability to understand heavenly language as his special gift.

16 K. J. Mathew, "Women in Church and Society", *Conviction, Journal of Bethel Bible College*, 1.2 (2013): 19.

17 K. J Mathew, "Women in Church and Society", 19.

18 Allan Anderson, *An Introduction to Pentecostalism*, (Cambridge: University Press, 2004), 19.

19 M. Stephen, *Towards a Pentecostal Theology and Ethics*, (Kottayam: Christhava Bodhi, 1999), 7.

The *Didache* and the *Shepherd of Hermas* recognize prophets who spoke in the Spirit. Bishop Clement of Rome tells the Corinthian believers as those who were filled with the Holy Spirit. Justin Martyr writes: 'Now it is possible to see women and men who possess gifts of the Spirit of God.' He also mentions of exorcism practiced by Christians of his time. Apart from these bishops, Bishop Irenaeus of Gaul, Clement of Alexandria provide significant information about spiritual lives of Christians in the latter part of the second century. None of these Church Fathers ever suggested that any of the gifts of the Spirit had ceased, or only men exercised them[20]

Throughout the first and second centuries, the gifts remained very important to the church. The church prior to A.D. 200 was charismatic. But when the church became established, hierarchy set in slowly and as a result the gifts of the Spirit slowly ceased or remained within the office of the bishops and priests.[21]

After the time of Origen (c. A.D. 184-254), most western church writers began to think that charismatic gifts were of the biblical times and had ceased. But among the Eastern Christians Pentecostal-like movement continued more vividly. The Eastern churches always recognized, and continued the experience throughout all the ages among them.[22] But slowly most of those who experienced the Holy Spirit baptism and tongues speech were secluded to the peripheries and as a result of the Christological conflicts of the time were branded as heretics.

According to William W. Menezies,

> There is an overwhelming evidence that the gift of the Spirit never did cease entirely. The pages of church history are punctuated with isolated and limited outpouring of the Spirit. None of these eruptions survived. Certainly the main stream of the Christian church did not embrace such

20 Ronald A. N. Kydd, *Charismatic Gifts in the Early Church*, (Massachusetts, Hendrickson Publishers, 1984), 4 and Allan Anderson, *An Introduction to Pentecostalism*, 20.

21 Simon Samuel, "The Charismatic and Pentecostal Movements and their Commitments to the Social Demands of the Gospel," 218.

22 Allan Anderson, *An Introduction to Pentecostalism*, 20.

occurrences, but the evidence remains that there has been at least a sprinkling of gifts of the Spirit throughout the centuries.[23]

## 1.3. The Migration of Syrian Christians from Persia to Malabar

In the early centuries the one fact which emerges with historical evidences is the connection of the Indian church with the church in the East: Syria, Mesopotamia, and Persia. The headquarters was in Antioch and Babylon. Most probably this was precipitated initially by two migrations of Syrian Christians to the Malabar Coast. The first immigration of a large colony of Christians of Persia to Malabar has taken place in the 4th century (345 A.D.) under the leadership of K'nai Thomman. To a certain extent the Persian immigration was beneficial to the Kerala Christians. But at the same time there are many who considered this relationship as a compromised one and a hurdle for the growth and development of the original Community. This relationship affected the Indian Christian Community in many areas of their spontaneous growth, pattern of thought, worship and life style, etc. Even the Syrians and Malabar Christians entered into matrimonial alliances and merged into a single community. The second migration had taken place during the 9th century (823 AD) and the tradition states that the migration rebuilt the town of Quilon in 823 AD. The contemporary evidence of this event is available in five copper plate, which are still in existence Kottayam and Thiruvalla.[24]

So from this migration it is possible that these Antiochean (Syrian) Charismatic Christians who migrated to Malabar had brought with them their priests and bishops and natives who converted into Christianity in India. Therefore, there is no point of suspecting the possibility of practising Pentecostal-like outpouring of the Holy Spirit including speaking in the tongues of angels and other ecstatic experiences. These are the clear evidences to argue for the

23 William W. Menzies, "The Reformed Roots of Pentecostalism", *AJPS* 9.2 (2006): 282.

24 K. M. George, *Christianity in India through the Centuries*, (Secunderabad: Authentic Books, 2007), 96-97.

view that St. Thomas Christians of Malankara in their earliest days practiced Pentecostal-like experience in their missionary activities.[25]

Besides these some New Testament scholars[26] like Gordan Fee, Robert Menzies, Stronstad, Keener and others argue that the earliest Christians were Charismatic and the early Christian movement was a charismatic Pentecostal-like movement which manifested the gift of the Holy Spirit such as speaking in tongues, healing, etc., in their ministry.

In the West, the Roman Catholic Church continued to deny the possibility of spiritual gifts. By the 11th century A.D., the Western church regarded charismatic manifestation as demonic. However, missionaries like Francis Xavier and Louis Bertrand said to have spoken in foreign languages they had never learned, and Xavier had the language of Angels and a ministry of healing. These were isolated and unusual events in the lives of saints and mystics and were not expected to be part of 'normal' church life. In fact these materials help us to see that the gifts of the spirit were very important features of Christianity and were practiced at least by a minority in the church.[27]

## 1.4. Fifteenth-Sixteenth Century: Arrival of Portuguese

The arrival of Portuguese Roman Catholic Christians in the sixteenth century, following Vasco de Gama's successful voyage to India in 1498, changed the face of Indian history as well as the history of Christianity. The Portuguese took over the complete control of the European trade in the sixteenth century but later the Dutch, the Danish, the English, and the French monopolized the trade as competitors.[28]

---

25 Simon Samuel, "The Charismatic and Pentecostal Movements and their Commitments to the Social Demands of the Gospel," 223 and Allan Anderson, *An Introduction to Pentecostalism*, 23.

26 Simon Samuel, "The Charismatic and Pentecostal Movements and their Commitments to the Social Demands of the Gospel," 223.

27 Allan Anderson, *An Introduction to Pentecostalism*, 23-24.

28 V. Mathew Kurien, "Syrian Christian and the Political Economy of Kerala", Indian Church History Review, Vol. XXVIII, (1994): 9.

Of all these western traders, only the Portuguese Roman Catholic Christians played a notable missionary activity under a system known as the 'Padroado'. The Portuguese zeal for spreading Roman Catholicism among the fishing community of the southeast and southwest coast of India was led by one of the first Jesuit missionaries to India, Francis Xavier. In addition to the Jesuits, several Catholic orders like Franciscans, the Dominicans and the Capuchins were actively involved in missionary enterprises.[29]

Though tremendous mission work had been done by the Portuguese Roman Catholic Christians in India, they found that St Thomas Christians followed the Syrian rite and received bishops from western Asia. St. Thomas Christians discovered that their rites are different from that of the Portuguese way of life. Throughout 16th century due to this difference, the relationship between the Portuguese and Indian churches remained tangled and tortuous.[30] Moreover, Portuguese brought out certain differences between Syrian and Western practice primarily in the liturgy, Roman doctrine and sacramental teaching. This affected their relationship, and it became strained. In order to settle the theological and liturgical issues, in the year 1599, Alexis de Menezes, the Archbishop of Goa, was determined to bring all the St Thomas Christians under the authority of the Pope through a historic Synod known as the Synod of Diamper. The compromise lasted only 54 years. In 1653, the Syrian Christians revolted against the Roman Catholics in what is called "the Coonen Cross" (Crooked Cross) incident. According to Roman Catholic historian this is the most famous event as well as one of the darkest years in the history of the Indian Church.[31] Due to this incident, nearly, one third of the Syrian churches returned to their older tradition and affiliated with the Patriarch of Antioch. A reform within the Syrian church much later in the 19th century brought a group out called the "Mar Thoma Church" in 1879. The Mar Thoma Church is more evangelical than the Indian Syrian Orthodox churches.

29 Joseph Thekkedath, *History of Christianity in* India, Vol. 2, (Bangalore: CHAI, 1988), 5-6, 55.

30 K. M. George, *Christianity in India through the Centuries*, 107-109.

31 Joseph Thekkedath, *History of Christianity in* India, 64-69.

## 1.5. Eighteenth Century: Arrival of Protestant Missionaries

It was in the early eighteenth century, while the Jesuits were still carrying on their work, the Protestant wing of Christianity and its missionaries arrived in India. The first Protestant mission in India was established in Tranquebar through the efforts of Bartholomew Ziegenbalg and Henry Pluetschau. They have been sent by King Frederick IV of Denmark. Ziegenbalg's translation of the Bible into Tamil was one of the major achievements made during those days. Robert De Nobili at Madurai immersed himself in the local Tamil culture making radical adaptations inculturating the Christian faith. Ziegenbalg at Tranquebar laid the foundations of an indigenous church by introducing a three–fold pietist model of mission consisting of Bible translation, schools and a simple expression of a local church.[32]

In 1800, British ruled India through East India Company. During this period, William Carey, a very remarkable Baptist missionary arrived in India. He made a great impact in the history of the church. Carey chose Serampore as the base for his mission work. He had been the leading spirit in the formation of the Baptist Missionary Society. One of his major contributions to the people of India was the translation of whole Bible in nearly forty languages.[33]

It was in this period the missionary movement began in England and this was one of the fruits of the evangelical revival, both within and without the Church of England. The English counterpart of the Pietist movement in Germany sent the first Protestant missionaries. In the last decade of the eighteenth century and the first two decades of the nineteenth, a number of missionary societies were founded, such as: the Baptist Missionary Society in 1792, the London Missionary Society in 1795 (LMS), the Church Missionary Society in 1799 (C.M.S), and the Wesleyan Methodist Missionary Society in 1813.[34]

---

32 Roger E. Hedlund, "Nationalism and the Indian Pentecostal Church of God", in *Indian Church History Review*, Vol. XXXII, (1998): 92.

33 A. C. George, *Trail Blazers for God: A History of the Assemblies of God of India*, (Bangalore: SABC Publications, 2004), 26.

34 C. B. Firth, *An Introduction to Indian Church History*, 145.

The above mentioned history shows that during those times women were expected to live a life of passive submission to the male dominated history and they were marginalized as far as leadership was concerned.[35] But still in many instances, women too played their roles as wives of most of the missionaries and some came as missionary.

Even the arrival of the Portuguese didn't make any changes in the upliftment of women. But in the last decade of eighteenth century, with the arrival of the Protestant missionaries, the situation began to change. Nineteenth century brought a great impact in various aspects on Indian women, especially the wives of protestant missionaries and missionary women. They began to make their mark in their respective missionary fields.[36] Many of these women missionaries tried to uplift the Indian women from their degraded position to a place of honour and respect. Ruth A. Tucker and Walter Liefeld out line this fact to show a connected history of the influence those missionary women had on Indian women in non-western lands.[37]

From the early decades of the 20th century, a large number of women's movements began to emerge. Most of the independent churches recognized the ministry of women in the church and their position. In Methodism and in the Holiness movement their various ministries were recognized. Phoebe Palmer and Nelly Terry were mighty preachers of this movement.[38]

A careful study on the brief history of the church down through the ages shows that women too made very valuable contributions to the growth of Indian Christianity and in the ministry of the early church. So, it must be kept in mind that without the involvement of these women, Christianity would not have become what is today.

---

35 Rosemary Ruether and Eleanor Mclaughlin, (eds.), *Women of Spirit: Female Leadership in the Jewish and Christian Traditions*, (New York: Simon and Schuster, 1979), 16-57.

36 Nancy A. Hardesty, *Women Called to Witness: Evangelical Feminism in the 19th Century*, (Knoxville: University of Tennessee Press, 1984), 9.

37 Ruth A.Tucker and Walter Liefeld, *Daughters of the Church: Women and Ministry from New Testament Times to the Present*, (Grand Rapids, Michigan: Zondervan Publishing House, 1984), 291.

38 K. J. Mathew, "Women in Church and Society", 18.

## 1.6. Beginning of Charismatic and Pentecostal-like Revival Movements in the West

### 1.6.1. Charismatic and Pentecostal-like Revival Movements: Differing Views

There are differences of opinion/views among the historians about the beginning of Charismatic and Pentecostal-like revival movements.

The classical view holds that the modern Pentecostal Movement had its beginning in 1901. Charles Fox Parham, a white American Holiness preacher, was the founder of the modern Pentecostal Movement.[39] Pentecostal historians, mainly from the west, generally agree that the modern Pentecostalism's immediate background in the west was in the 19th century Holiness movement and German Pietism. The members of these movements which include women such as Phoebe Palmer and others emphasized the importance of a personal experience of God or a 'new birth' in the Holy Spirit over and above mere head-knowledge, as part of their argument for the ministry of women in the church. Essentially, however, the Pentecostal movement began as an emotional and theologically more experimental wing of the Holiness Movement.[40]

Scholars note that the Modern Pentecostalism arose from multiple revivals such as Methodist-Holiness, the Reformed revivalism of Jonathan Edwards, and the Oberlin Perfectionism of revivalists like Charles Finney, the Keswick and Healing Movements of the 19th century England and America played an important influence in the rise of early modern Pentecostalism as a Movement. Such Evangelical awakening and the Holiness Movement of the second half of the nineteenth century form the West proceeds the background of the Modern Pentecostal Movement.[41]

Though, simultaneously there were spontaneous revivals in many parts of the world including India, modern Pentecostalism has an immediate background in the nineteenth century Holiness

39 V. V. Thomas, *Dalit Pentecostalism: Spirituality of the Empowered Poor*, (Bangalore: Asian Trading Corporation, 2008), 35.

40 Simon Samuel, "The Charismatic and Pentecostal Movements and their Commitments to the Social Demands of the Gospel," 221.

41 V. V. Thomas, *Dalit Pentecostalism: Spirituality of the Empowered Poor*, 37.

movement and German Pietism. An even more important influence in the shaping of Pentecostalism was the Holiness movement. Charles G. Finney was the leading Holiness preacher in this period.[42]

Nils Bloch Hoell, a well known historian of Pentecostalism, making his observation on the revival movements which preceded the Pentecostal Movement, says that, Methodism, Pietism, and American revivalism prepared the way for the Pentecostal Movement, which emerged in America in the early 20th century. England and America played an important influence in the rise of early modern Pentecostalism as a movement.[43]

As noted earlier the Modern Pentecostal Movement is the outcome of the various revivals that took place during 18th and 19th centuries. Frank Sandford, a Baptist pastor, experienced the spirit baptism in 1894, through his experience of sanctification in the Holiness movement. His main impact was on Charles Parham of Topeka, Kansas and a few women like Agnes Ozman, Mary Arthur, Anna Hall, Mabel Smith, and Jessie Brown who underwent a similar experience. One of the leaders of the Welsh revival (1904) was Florae Evans, a young girl.[44] At the outbreak of the modern Pentecostal movement in 1901, it was Agnes Ozman, a young girl who began to speak in tongues. Charles F. Parham was the key person. He founded a Bible School in Houston, Texas where one of the strange attendees was William Joseph Seymour, a black African-American. He was permitted to sit outside the class room and listen to the lectures. After his training in Parham's School (Parham later on in his life turned out to be a strong advocate of white racism), Seymour went to Azusa Street in Los Angeles where the modern Pentecostalism is believed to have its birth in the west. Here various women, both black and white, also figured prominently.[45]

---

42 V. V. Thomas, *Dalit Pentecostalism: Spirituality of the Empowered Poor*, 37.

43 Allan Anderson, *An Introduction to Pentecostalism*, 27, 34, Nils Bloch Hoell, *The Pentecostal Movement: Its Origin, Development and Distinctive Character,* (London: George Allen & Unwin Ltd., 1964), 67.

44 Barbara L. Cavaness, "*Leadership Attitudes and the Ministry of Single Women in Assemblies of God Missions,*" edited by Estrelda Alexander and Amos Yong, (Oregon: Pickwick Publications, 2009), 119.

45 Harvey Cox, *Fire from Heaven*, 58, 79.

## 1.7. Beginning of Charismatic and Pentecostal-like Revival Movements in India

### 1.7.1. Beginnings of Charismatic and Pentecostal- like Revival Movements in South India (Nineteenth Century)

The second half of the 19th century witnessed strong missionary activities in different parts of India. The Syrian Christian Community had recorded instances of revivals since the second half of 19th century. Protestant missionaries were actively involved in bringing reforms among the Malabar and other South Indian Christians. Some of the CMS missionaries like Thomas Norton, Benjamin Bailey, and Henry Baker worked closely with the Syrian church and taught at the Old Seminary in Kottayam founded by John Munore in 1813. Their cooperation and teaching paved the way for a revision of liturgy and removal of corruptions and unbelief.[46] This process flashed of an awakening in the Malankara Syrian Orthodox church in 1837 especially under the leadership of a 'Malankara Martin Luther' by name Malpan Abraham (Malpan means Professor) of Maramon, who was teacher of the Old Seminary at that time. As a result, the reformed Mar Thoma Syrian Christian church of Malabar originated.[47] It is from this strand of Malankara Christianity, early Pentecostalism began in Kerala.

The three stalwarts of native Pentecostalism in Kerala and their leaders and laymen came from this community. Pastor K. E. Abraham, Pastor P. M. Samuel and Pastor K. C. Cherian were very active in church activities. According to Edwin Orr, due to the instances of revivals new groups professing evangelical faith emerged from among the Syrian Christian Community. These revival and reformation broke out by numerous native missionaries like Justus

---

46 Simon Samuel, "The Charismatic and Pentecostal Movements and their Commitments to the Social Demands of the Gospel", 224.

47 Daniel Jeyaraj, "The History of Christianity in India: An overview from a Protestant Perspective" in *Missiology for the 21st Century: South Asian Perspectives*, ed. Roger Hedlund and Bhakiaraj (New Delhi: ISPCK, 2004), 195-211.

Joseph, K. V. Simon, Mammen Upadesi and many other known and unknown revival preachers (men and women) of that time.[48]

The Syrian church always had openness to the missionaries from the West. However, they did not allow them to contaminate their socio-religious and ecclesiastical practices. To substantiate this, I would like to illustrate with one example prior to the origin of Pentecostalism in India.

As India became a British colony, evangelical missionaries from different parts of European countries entered in Kerala. The Syrian metropolitans did allow the missionaries to preach in their churches as long as they did not interfere with their own traditions and liturgical practices. However, they did control their activities. The mutual understanding with Western missionaries especially Anglicans, extend their cooperation in the area of Bible translation, production of literature, and given permission for them to conduct evangelistic work and revival meetings after the regular *Korbana* (liturgical service) in the church. Metropolitan, Mar Dionysius sought the help of Claudius Buchanan to get the Bible in Syriac version. In 1806, Buchanan get 100 copies of the Syriac Bible printed. The Bible in Syriac language was the first printed copies that this community had. During this time Mar Dionysius also got the Syriac version translated into the local language, Malayalam, and got it printed by the help of Buchanan. Another Metropolitan, by name Mathews Mar Athanasius encouraged western missionaries to visit and preach in their churches but this did not last long since the revival broke out that Syrian church could not tolerate. After this event in 1830 the Syrian Metropolitan Chepad Mar Dionysius (1827-1856) prohibited the work of the western missionaries through an encyclical.[49]

As a consequence, a number of Syrian Christians got enlightened; many of them left the church and joined the Church Missionary Society. The major split happened about half a century

48 Paulson Pulikottil, "As East and West Met in God's Own Country: Encounter of Western Pentecostalism with Native Pentecostalism in Kerala," in *AJPS*, 5/1 (2002): 7.

49 Paulson Pulikottil, "As East and West Met in God's Own Country: Encounter of Western Pentecostalism with Native Pentecostalism in Kerala," 12.

later by the formation of the Mar Thoma church, a reformed Syrian church in 1876. The effect of this desertion and division is that the Syrian Christian community have to keep a distance from the western missionaries. In this situation the Syrian Christians recognized the importance to maintain their identity and to protect their socio-religious and ecclesiastical space from invasion than spiritual revival. Spiritual revival at the cost of ethnic and Ecclesiastical identity was not negotiable.[50]

The seeds of these movements can be traced to the Christian converts from Tirunelveli and Travancore in 1860s and 1870s by the influence of missionaries from Pietistic and CMS background. These awakening marked as the hope for the outpouring of the Holy Spirit, restoration of the Spiritual gifts, etc. K. E Abraham, quoted in his writings, *History of Pentecostalism in Kerala*, "Those who had these experiences in those days did not realise that they were speaking in tongues as they were endowed with the Holy Spirit; they did not have sufficient knowledge of scripture in this matter." One such revival began at Tirunelveli under the leadership of John Aroolappan, a trained Anglican catechist. The charismatic phenomena in this revival included prophecy, *glossolalia*, interpretation of tongues, dreams, signs in heaven, falling down, conviction of sin, evangelism, etc.[51]

During this period we can identify that there is a tendency for independent movements within the church. People were experiencing a kind of suffocation within the established structures. This revival took an indigenous turn, as a result there were men and women involved in the evangelistic outreach. On one occasion, these revived Christians came out of the traditional control of "native" churches and clergy by paternalistic missionary societies. Through the influence of the Aroolappen family and their followers, the movement spread westward a decade later into nearby Travancore among CMS congregations and those of the Syrian church of Malabar and met

50 Paulson Pulikottil, "As East and West Met in God's Own Country: Encounter of Western Pentecostalism with Native Pentecostalism in Kerala," 12.

51 G. B. McGee and S. M. Burges, 'India' in *The New International Dictionary of Pentecostal Charismatic Movements*, edited by Stanley M. Burges, (Grand Rapids, Michigan: Zondervan Publishing House, 2001), 118.

with considerable success. Prominent among the two leaders are Kudarapallil Thommen and a Brahmin convert Justus Joseph.[52]

### 1.7.2. Charismatic and Pentecostal-like Outpouring Revivals across North East and North India

Towards the close of the 19th century (in March 1905) a great revival occurred among tribal peoples in the Khassia Hills in the North East, at Welsh Presbyterian mission stations and also this Pentecostal fire sparkled in Maharashtra at Pandita Ramabai's Mukti Mission at Kedgaon.[53] The emerging evidence of manifestation of the Holy Spirit was reported at Zenana Bible and medical orphanage at Manmad and CMS boarding school at Mumbai with several Pentecostal-like Phenomena. In all these cases they experienced Charismatic gifts (Prophecy, *glossolalia*, interpretation of tongues, etc.).[54] This movement received greater criticism. As a result they even set aside the traditional and hierarchical pattern of worship. In these revivals meetings all those who had the experiences of baptism of the Holy Spirit, spoke in other tongues was not considered as a "Bible evidence" doctrine, later popularly called the "initial evidence" and later it served as one of the earliest expositions of Pentecostal faith and mission. As tradition says, and in the light of article on *The Holy Spirit Led Mission in North India* by James Massey, there is a strong possibility of the arrival of St. Thomas coming first to Punjab and Holy Spirit directed him to Pentecostal-like mission in the churches of St. Thomas Christians and later it was destroyed by the Buddhist kings. After the arrival of modern Protestant missionaries and with

52 G. B. McGee and S. M. Burges, "India", The New International Dictionary of Pentecostal and Charismatic Movements, 119.

53 Helen Kooiman Hosier, *100 Christian Women Who Changed the 20th Century*, (Secunderbad: OM Books International, 2000), 257, Donna Kafer *Women of Courage*, (Orlando: Bridge-Logos, 2007), 75.

54 Gary B. McGee, "'Latter Rain' Falling in the East: Early-Twentieth-Century Pentecostalism in India and The Debate over Speaking in Tongues" in *Church History: Studies in Christianity and Culture*, 68/3 (1999): 653.

their effort it turned as a centre of missionary activity in the North-west of Punjab.[55]

In 1907, Alfred Garr and Lillian Gar, spirit filled missionaries arrived in Calcutta, with their experiences of the outpouring of the Holy Spirit from Azusa street revival, and the influence of the revival in Calcutta continued to spread as Gar travelled across the country holding services and presenting classical Pentecostal doctrine of Baptism in the Holy Spirit. This paved the way to create a new dimension among the Charismatic Pentecostal-like movement in India. About the same time the "fire of the Spirit" fell on the Elliot Road orphanage in Kolkata, where a Methodist missionary, Fannie Simpson, ministered. Though, Simpson had been expelled from the Methodist church, she remained in India as an independent Pentecostal missionary and established the girls' orphanage at Purulia.[56] From that time onwards certain quarters of the Pentecostal movement asserted that speaking in tongues are the sole evidence of the baptism of the Holy Spirit. This was the position taken by classical Pentecostals in the West and in the south India in the early days of the movement. Thus, speaking in tongue became the hall mark of a Pentecostal. In the fall of 1907 the ministries of Gar (presenting the classical Pentecostal doctrine of baptism in the Holy Spirit) received greater criticism; even this was questioned by Minnie Abrams and others who objected to their absolute indispensability for Spirit baptism. (Minnie Abrams, an associate of Ramabai and some time Methodist missionary).

Despite of this dispute, the largest number of veteran missionaries in any one country to embrace the Pentecostal gifts including speaking in tongues lived in India by 1910. Among them a good number was women, including Minnie Abrams, Kate Knight, Laura Gardner, Eveline A. Luce, Agnes and many others. Women made notable contributions that included theological and missiological reflection. For example, Kate Knight (CMA) became an

55 James Massey, 'Holy Spirit led Mission in North India' in *Missiology for the 21st Century: South Asian Perspectives*, ed. Roger E. Hedlund and Paul Joshua Bhakiaraj (Delhi: ISPCK, 2004), 254.

56 Simon Samuel, "The Charismatic and Pentecostal Movements and their Commitments to the Social Demands of the Gospel," 228.

outspoken apologist for the movement, while Abrams also contributed to such reflection; Abrams recruited six new women missionaries to Mukti Mission. Some of these early missionaries became associated with the AG church when it was organised in 1914. Most of the missionaries, however, remained with their agencies, possibly due to an unwillingness to accept the classical Pentecostal view of tongues or lose their current missionary status.[57]

According to Burgess and McGee, mission publications carried stories of Pentecostal–like experiences across India among the Anglicans (CMS), American Baptist Mission, CMA, LMS, Young Men's and women's Christian Associations, Methodists and others. All these denominations captured the attention of Pentecostal-like outpourings, and charismatic phenomena. These Spirit filled miraculous works and charismatic experiences served as a prelude to the larger ecumenical gathering of foreign mission societies (International Mission Conference) in 1910, known as the Edinburg 1910, a fact which did not receive much space within the mainstream of Christian historiography.[58]

## 1.8. The Impact of Early Missionaries for the Expansion of Modern Pentecostalism in India

The brief summary of the origin of Pentecostalism in India helps us to understand that the South India was more responsive than North India to Pentecostalism. North India was one of the hardest mission fields and this was proved by the efforts of early missionaries. While missionaries in the South experienced considerable growth, those in the North saw little fruit for their labours.

Because of difficulties faced in evangelising North India, early Pentecostal missionaries turned to establishing institutions such as orphanages, industrials schools, elementary schools, correspondence schools, radio programs, leper asylums, and dispensaries. The AG church has the most extensive system of institutional works including an orphanage and girls' school at Bettiah; a girls' orphanage at Purulia,

57 G. B. McGee and S. M. Burgess, "India," 120.

58 Simon Samuel, "The Charismatic and Pentecostal Movements and their Commitments to the Social Demands of the Gospel," 229.

a leper work at Uska Bazar, begun in 1911 by Minnie Abrams; the best known AG church work in all of India, by Mark and Huldah Buntain in Kolkata, beginning in 1953 with the "Mission of Mercy" which now feeds over 20,000 hungry mouths each day.[59]

## 1.9. Development and Growth of Pentecostalism in Kerala

The development and growth of Pentecostalism in Kerala is the product of the labours of many men and women missionaries that God used to spread the Pentecostal doctrine and established churches in the region. Therefore, it is necessary to mention briefly the life and activities of some of the pioneers, who are only representatives of scores of people who became instrumental in laying the foundation of the Pentecostal movement in the state of Travancore (Kerala).

### 1.9.1. George Berg

The Pentecostal message from the West arrived in Kerala through the visit of George Berg, the American missionary of German descent. He arrived in Bangalore in 1908. He came to Kerala for the first time in 1909 and preached in a Brethren convention in Kerala. Berg visited Kerala again in 1910 but he had to confront tremendous opposition from the Brethren missionaries forcing him to organise meeting of his own. Berg's third visit to Kerala was in 1911 in the company of an Anglo Indian missionary called Charles Cumins, and two American expatriate Brethren missionaries Aldiwinkle and Bouncil. They received the baptism in the Holy Spirit at a revival meeting of Thomas Barrett in 1908. Thereafter they had become Pentecostal missionaries. However, the first Pentecostal congregation was formed through the tire-less efforts of Berg in Kerala only in 1911. This gathering was among the first generation Christians. A young evangelist of the Marthoma Church, Pandalam Mathai and an active member of the CMS, Dr. Oommen Mammen became

---

59 G. B. McGee and S. M. Burgess, "India," 124 and T. J. Samuel, "The Origin and Growth of Assemblies of God Church in Kerala," in *Assemblies of God Doodhan*, (1995): 8-9.

Pentecostals through the influence of George Berg. Berg was the first missionary to reach out to the natives who did not speak English.[60]

### 1.9.2. Robert F. Cook

Robert Cook, an American Missionary was one of the first missionaries to come to India with the Pentecostal message. He played a major role in the establishment of Pentecostal churches in Travancore and other places in South India. He came to India in October 1913 together with his wife Anna and their two daughters, Blossom and Dorothy, to work as independent "faith missionaries" following the trails of Berg. They lived in South Indian city of Bangalore and started working in association with Berg. Soon he was able to start an English worship in Frazer Town. The death of his wife Anna in 1917 shattered him, for she was a great asset to his ministry. His prayer for a dedicated partner like Anna was answered the following year, when he met and married Bertha Fox who was working in India as a Methodist missionary.[61]

By this time some of the congregations that Berg had founded joined the mission of Cook. At this stage, initially Cook worked with George Berg and his former colleagues who were expatriate missionaries. During that time he worked in Bangalore and visited various parts of Travancore. Cook was able to establish many churches particularly among the low caste Hindus and Christians in Kerala.[62]

Later Cook had become a missionary affiliated with the AG church in U.S.A. Until 1926 Cook was leading a new Pentecostal denomination by the name South India Full Gospel Church. Later on he left AG church and moved to Chengannur in Kerala and founded the Mount Zion Bible Institute at Mulakuzha in June 1927 with the help of two native school teachers named T. M.Varghese and K. E. Abraham, who later became Charismatic preachers. Later K. C. Cherian also joined them. T. M. Varghese later became the leader of Church of God (full Gospel) denomination of the Indian

---

60 Paulson Pullikottil, "As East and West Met in God's Own Country: Encounter of Western Pentecostalism with Native Pentecostalism in Kerala," 8.

61 A.C. George, "Pentecostal Beginning in Travancore, South India," 225-227.

62 J. Yesunatha Das, "A Dalit Tribute to Robert F. Cook: The Pentecostal Pioneer in India," Unpublished Work, 1-8.

Pentecostal Church centred at Mulakuza. Later in 1930s, Cook joined with Varghese, served together and founded the Indian Pentecostal Church (IPC) at Kumbanad near Maramon.[63]

### 1.9.3. Mary Chapman

Another missionary who came to India, who later became the founder of AG Pentecostal denomination was Mary Weems Chapman. She travelled extensively throughout India and settled in Madras in 1915. Later she moved to Kerala to help the flood victims. The need and urgency of the work in Travancore prompted her to move to Trivandrum (now known as Tiruvananthapuram) in 1921. Through her influence, Miss Aldwinkle, an independent missionary, joined the AG church fellowship. Chapman and Aldwinkle work together and established Pentecostal work in several places. During this period Robert Cook was working in Kottarakara. In 1923, Mary Chapman worked along with a British AG church missionary, Spencer May who came to Kerala. In the same year they published the first Malayalam Pentecostal magazine call *Pentecostal Trumpet.* Even though, Chapman laboured in Kerala only for about ten years, she was able to lay a solid foundation for the AG church work. Following year Chapman went to Kollam (Quilon) for a brief period and finally came to Mavelikara and laboured there until she was called to her heavenly home on November 27, 1927. During her period of work in Kerala, God gave her a band of young partners in the ministry. They were, C. Manasseh, A. J. John, P. V. John and K. E. Abraham, etc. Her contribution to Pentecostalism in Travancore will always be remembered.[64]

### 1.9.4. John H. Burgess

In 1924, William M. Fox, foreign Mission Secretary of the AG church (U.S.A.) came to Kerala to conduct revival meetings. He soon recognized the need and progress of the work to have an additional missionaries and Indian workers in Kerala. He recommended that

63 Simon Samuel, "The Charismatic and Pentecostal Movements and their Commitments to the Social Demands of the Gospel," 229.

64 C. Kunjummen, "The Early History", in *Assemblies of God* Doodhan, 4.

a missionary be commissioned and sent to Travancore to have a Bible School for training future workers. The young man chosen for this task was John Burgess who arrived in Travancore (Kerala) in 1926. Chapman and Burgess work together in Mavelikara. In June 1927, they established the first AG Bible School, i.e., Bethel Bible Institute at Mavelikara, which was later, shifted to Punalur. This is the earliest Bible College of AG outside the US. The enormous way of contribution of John Burges and his wife Bernice in developing Bethel Bible School will always be remembered.[65]

Other than these, there were few others who contributed behind for the development of this mission work, such as Miss Mildred C. Ginn, C. T. Maloney, A. C. Samuel and his wife, Miss Lydia H. Graner, Pastor Kunjummen, Rev. Ernest A. Sorbo and Dr. Carl D. Holleman. Another AG missionary Martha M. Kucera came to India in 1928 and had been working in Trivandrum and nearby places.[66]

## 1.10. The Formation of Various Pentecostal Movements

In this section, I would like to draw some of the historical glimpses of the Pentecostal movements.

In the 1920's there was an active evangelistic church in Northern Travancore, by the name of Christ Church, under the leadership of C. V. Tharappan. In the mean time Robert F. Cook came back from the United States, now as a missionary of the AG church, and an administrative unity was established between the churches under the leadership of Cook (South India Full Gospel Church of God) and those under Indian leaders (South India Pentecostal Church). In 1926, SIPC and SIFGC merged to form the united church called the Malankara Pentecostal Church with R. F. Cook as President and K. E. Abraham as vice-President. Until 1929, Pentecostal churches though they were known by different names they had very close relationships and worked together. However, this did not last long. In the same year, Malankara

65 Saju, *Kerala Pentekostu Charithram*, (Kottayam: Good News Publication, 1994), 60.

66 Issac V. Mathew, "Theological Education in the Malayalam District of A.G.," in *SIAG Malayalam District Council Souvenir* (2000): 53-55.

Pentecostal Church split from the AG church. In January 1930, the former South India Pentecostal Church (SIPC) separated from the union (Malankara Pentecostal Church) under the leadership of K.E. Abraham.[67]

All the Pentecostal churches were against organised administration in the beginning. They believed in the freedom of local churches. But by the middle of this decade we find them taking an organisational nature. The work of South India Pentecostal Church began to flourish outside Kerala and even to the northern parts of India. On April 9, 1934, the church was named as the Indian Pentecostal Church of God (IPC). The Malankara Full Gospel Church under the leadership of Cook joined with the Church of God, Tennessee (Cleveland, USA) in 1936 and took the name Church of God (Full Gospel) in India.[68]

## 1.11. The Beginning of the Assemblies of God in Kerala

The beginning of Pentecostal work in South India is connected between the ministry of Mary Chapman and Robert Cook who did pioneering ministry in different parts of India. The AG church in Travancore did not come into existence with some organizational structure until 1929, although the Pentecostal message and experience came to Travancore at least two decades earlier. The first AG church district to be organized was the "South West District Council." The "Madras State District Council" was formed in 1948 and its name was later changed into Tamil Nadu District Council. It became a registered body in 1951. Presently the South India Assemblies of God consists of 8 districts.[69]

### 1.11.1. The Role of the Native Leaders

It has been mentioned earlier that all western missionaries worked with native missionaries who had charismatic figure, great vision

---

67 George Oommen, "Robert Cook: His Role in Shaping the beginnings of Pentecostalism in Kerala," unpublished paper presented at the Faculty Seminar in NTC, Dehradun on July 15, 2013, 3.

68 George Oommen, "Robert Cook: His Role in Shaping the beginnings of Pentecostalism in Kerala," 8.

69 T. J. Samuel, "The Origin and Growth of Assemblies of God in Kerala," 8.

and commitment and who would be a tremendous responsible for the spread of Pentecostalism in Travancore and elsewhere. Among them some of them are well known but many others remaining in obscurity. However, it is my immense task to highlight some of the native leaders and their wives and good number of single missionary women and the women evangelists who paid a great price to spread the flames of revival for the growth and development of Pentecostal movement and contributed immeasurably and played pivotal role towards the expansion of this movement.

God, in His mercy, choose Pastor K. E. Abraham as the founder of the Indian Pentecostal Church of God. God raised other ministers also in His fellowship such as K. C. Oommen, P. T. Chacko, K. C. Cherian, K. M. Zachariah, P. T. Varghese and several others. By the end of 1926 there were over 20 local churches and 25 ministers in this fellowship. Even along with K. C. Cherian, P. M. Samuel, M. K. Chacko, P. T. Chacko, T. G. Oommen, C. K. Daniel, P. L. Paramjyothy, V. T. Joseph, M. V. Chacko, P. M. Philip, T. S. Abraham their wives also took equal responsibilities for the Gospel. They paid a great price for the cause of this new faith. Annamma Cherian (wife of K. C. Cherian) became sick because of the unfavourable climate and starvation. Even in her sick bed, she never grumbled rather was a tremendous support and source of encouragement to her husband. There are many other elders who are alive and are still labouring for God.

In the lives of many servants of God, their wives worked with them shoulder to shoulder. But in a male dominated society women's (whether they are ordinary woman or pastor's wives) role and contribution towards the growth and development of the church is not highlighted. They are seen as someone who is inferior. Due to this reason very often their names and their roles in history of the church had been either hidden or given as passive remark. We should acknowledge the reality that women were also instrumental in laying the foundation for building and establishing God's Kingdom.

### *1.11.1.1. K. E. Abraham*

K. E. Abraham received the Pentecostal experience on 22 April 1923 at the home of C. Manasseh, an A. G. Pastor who spread the Pentecostal message in Southern parts of Travancore. Abraham narrates his own experience,

> "While we were praying, Bro. Manasseh laid his hands up on my head and prayed; All of a sudden I experienced the passing of a current through my body. By the power of the spirit my body began to shiver.....I was overwhelmed with joy and began to praise God..... My tongue so moved that I was unable to praise God in my mother tongue...... following that I spoke again in tongues."[70]

In course of time Abraham focused his work on building up of indigenous churches. Meanwhile, many independent local churches were started in Kerala. In the beginning they had no special name. When they faced the need for marriage registration, they choose the name "South Indian Pentecostal Church of God." Abraham was later acknowledged and recognized as a founder and chief architect of the Indian Pentecostal Church, which is one of the largest Pentecostal churches in India today. Monthly fellowship meeting began in 1924. The first general convention of this fellowship was held at Ranni during April 1-5, 1925. Pastor K. E. Abraham, the president of the fellowship, was the main speaker along with Pastor A. J. John.[71]

On May 1, 1930, Pastor K. E. Abraham and his family moved their residence from Mulakuzha to Kumbanad. Obeying the inspiration God gave him, K. E. Abraham started Hebron Bible School in June 1930. During and after the lifetime of Pastor Abraham, his wife actively worked in the spiritual matters of the church as the president of the I. P. C. sisters organization for a long time. In 1975, Mrs. K. E. Abraham started Hebron Ladies Bible School. The work of the church began to spread in Kerala and other parts of India. In 1934, the name of the church was changed to "India Pentecostal Church of God." Pastor K. E. Abraham is well remembered as an "apostle" that God raised to provide leadership to that movement

---

70 A. C. George, "Pentecostal Beginning in Travancore, South India," 231.

71 Yesukristhuvinte Eliya Dassan: Autobiography of Pastor K. E. Abraham, 93.

and to become blessing to thousands of people through his ministry in India and across the globe.[72]

### 1.11.1.2. P. T. Chacko

Pastor P. T. Chacko and his family worked in Andhra Pradesh in 1936. He worked with Pastor P. M. Samuel, Bro. P. M. Thomas and others. P. T. Chacko trained Pastors P. M. Philip, T. K. Thomas, P. L. Paramjyothi and P. J. Thomas and many others. In 1940, they moved to Secunderabad and started a Bible School there, teaching evangelists to serve the Lord in Andhra Pradesh. His wife Annamma Chacko had been a tremendous help for evangelistic work. She preached to the women in English and Telugu. She was a prayer warrior and was never idle for the Lord.[73]

### 1.11.1.3. K. C. Oommen

Pastor K. C. Oommen began his Christian life as a member of the Brethren church. Later, he was miraculously healed from a severe stomach pain by the prayer of Pastor Robert Cook. Following his healing he joined the Pentecostal church. Active in the Church ministry and worked very sincerely and actively with Pastor K. E. Abraham. God used native missionaries to plant churches and spread the Pentecostal message all over Travancore.[74]

### 1.11.1.4. C. Manasseh

Manasseh is regarded as a pioneer of AG church work in the southern Travancore. His wife, Shelal, proved her God given talent and potentiality as a renowned woman preacher during those time. More than a woman missionary, Shelal was a woman who made friendship with the public and won their respect and love. Her well-respected life made Manasseh to become more successful in his ministry. Manasseh served as a volunteer evangelist with the London Missionary Society for some time, but was excommunicated from that church due to

---

72 T. Valsan Abraham, 'Trumpet: Faith of our Fathers,' *IPC 75, Platinum Jubilee edition*, Vol. 9, 1991, 3.

73 T. Valsan Abraham, "Trumpet: Faith of our Fathers", 3.

74 Yesukristhuvinte Eliya Dassan : Autobiography of Pastor K. E. Abraham, 93.

his reform ideas. But God brought him get in contact with Miss Aldwinkle, a Pentecostal missionary resided in Tanjore that led him into the Pentecostal faith. He was baptised in water and later received the Spirit baptism. Soon he started evangelistic work in his own native place. God used him effectively in several places. In 1922 he began the first AG church in Konniyoor. He was one of the leading workers in that area. When Mary Chapman moved to Trivandrum, they worked closely together in South Travancore. From 1922 to 1938 Manasseh was the pastor of the Melapuram church. At present this district has over 250 churches and well established Bible College called Southern Bible College.[75]

### *1.11.1.5. A. C. Samuel*

Another Servant of God who was chosen by God to build up the AG church work in Travancore was A. C. Samuel. His parents were members of the Brethren church. For a while he was actively involved in the youth wing of the Brethren church in Travancore. This gave him an opportunity to be a witness for the Lord in his native place and other places. He was influenced by the life style and the nature of charismatic work done by Robert Cook. Young Samuel was attracted to the Pentecostal faith. In 1924 when William Faux came to Travancore and conducted special meetings, in one of those meetings, he received the baptism in the Spirit, and soon he started working with Cook in several places along with his friends K. C. Oommen and K. E. Abraham. This resulted in the establishment of several Pentecostal Churches in central Travancore. From 1927 he pastored a church at Anjilithanam.[76]

Samuel came into contact with the AG church missionary, Martha M. Kucera when she came to the Trivandrum area. Miss Kucera came to India in 1928 and had been working in Trivandrum and nearby places before Samuel came to Trivandrum. Their joint efforts resulted in the formation of many churches. During those days Pastor Samuel was recognized in many ways, and held numerous titles such as, "first man" in relation to the AG church work in South India,

75 A. C. George, "Pentecostal beginnings in Travancore, South India," 231-232.

76 Saju, *Kerala Penthekosthu Charithram*, 68.

first Indian to be ordained by the AG church leadership in Ceylon (Sri Lanka) in 1935, first General Superintendent of the Malayalam District (1947) and the first Indian to go to USA to represent the AG churches in India (accompanied by Pastor C. Kunjummen, the District Secretary). He also held several other positions.[77] P. D. Johnson, P. N. Zachariah, etc. There are many great servants of God who contributed and dedicated their lives for the growth of the Kingdom of God. There are women ministers and lay leaders who denied all the promises of life just to please God and build the church. We can't forget the valuable service and contributions.

### *1.11.1.6. Ponnamma Sanyasini*

Ponnamma Sanyasini, a single woman is living in the city of Bangalore, who is over 90 years of age, an evangelist who visited a number of churches in South India and left a great impression upon many people. There is a lot of others who served and still serving the church and the Lord sincerely and silently without any motivation for earthly rewards. That list is too long. It is not just a group, it is a crowd.

The growth and development of AG church must be seen as the history of great men and women whose lives have witnessed and who were in the forefront in evangelistic ministry. The history of the AG church in South India is the history of a few notable exceptions of strong dedication, toil, and sacrifices. The name enlisted above are a few examples of the many, whom are deserved to be noticed and who obeyed the heavenly calling and did their maximum for the growth of God's Kingdom in this part of the world.

In the following chapter, I will be exploring the role and contribution of women in the life of the AG church.

77 L. Sam, "AG. Charithra Rekhakal," in *SIAG Malayalam District Council Souvenir*, 21-33.

Chapter 2

# The Role of Women Leaders in the Origin and Growth of the Pentecostal Movement in Kerala

## Introduction

In Indian historiography, whether secular or Christian, the people of inferior rank, especially women, were not given due attention or recognition. Quite often, women's voice was ignored or silenced by those who wrote history. This was the case in the writing of the history of Christianity too. Hence, the main purpose of this chapter is to make an attempt to re-read and re-write the place of women and their contribution in the history of Christianity from a woman's perspective. For this task the feminist and womanist historiographers have produced tools for a critical reading of the text in order to interpret and understand Christianity in the scope of digging out the role and contribution of women and also see the equality of women and men in Christian leadership. They believe that this is necessary for a fuller picture of the history of Christianity. If not, the history will be a lopsided history.

There are two major sections in this chapter. In the first section I will look at the need and importance of a revisionist feminist historiography and in the second section my task is to discover the women's place and role throughout the history of the church, the place and contribution of women in the church at large in India and the ministerial role of women in the Pentecostal movement and their contribution to the church in Kerala specially in Kannur District.

## 2.1. The Need and Importance of a Revisionist Feminist Historiography

One of the major tasks of women historians and researchers in historiography is to re-read, deconstruct and re-construct the history written by men from a feminist/womanist perspective. It is impossible to deny the fact that the women's story are kept aside from the main stream of the society. Large proportions of women throughout history have not been granted their due voice, position and space whether in the Bible or in the other writings. In order to render justice to all sections of the society especially to women who were victims of patriarchy, the pioneer feminists took up the tools of critical feminist historical inquiry and dared to examine those truths. They sought explanations for the things which puzzled them.[78] As a result feminist historians have come to the forefront, seeing the exclusion of women and their experiences. The male-centered mainline historiography has forced the feminist critics to enter into the arena.

Feminist historians and theologians, such as Elizabeth Schussler Fiorenza, Elizabeth Cady Stanton, Sarah Grimke, Mary Daly developed a feminist approach to the interpretation of religion, history in general and of the Bible in particular. They challenge not only the androcentric reality construction in the language but also seek to move from androcentric texts to egalitarian- historical contexts. Androcentrism characterizes a mind set, and patriarchy represents a social-cultural system in which a few men have power over other men, women, children, etc. Their approach challenges the cultural aspects such as textual interpretations, historical reconstruction and

78 Dorothy C. Bass, "Women's Studies and Biblical Studies: An Historical Perspective," *JSOT*, Vol. 22 (1982): 6.

the use of language.[79] They challenge the assumption of women's cultural marginality and religious subordination. Thus, feminist theologians and historians launched a revisionist historiography and hermeneutics.

There are many approaches of rewriting history from a feminist perspective. Some of them a) Not only seek to recover forgotten traditions about women by removing the layers of centuries of androcentric interpretation that cover up the supposed involvement of women in the history of the church. Women scholars have shown that the history have either neglected women's presence in the mission or distorted the place and role of women in the history of Christianity,[80] b) Others seek to recover works written by women in order to restore critical attention to female voices and intellectual traditions, c) Yet others focus on early Christian history, concentrate on the ideological inscriptions of androcentric texts, and shift attention from the androcentric text to women as the leading subjects, etc.[81]

There are a few who see the scripture and liturgy too as male-dominated. So they change the exclusive language used in Scripture too as the traditional theology and the structure of the church are extremely examined to grant dignity and rights of women in the church.[82]

Looking at history from a below perspective, the existing record of history is evidently a male-streamed history and it is one sided. This made feminists weary about the way women's roles have been down played and deliberately ignored. They criticised the history

---

79 Elisabeth Schüssler Fiorenza, "Feminist Theology and New Testament Interpretation," *JSOT*, 22 (1982): 32.

80 Karen Jo Torjesen, "Reconstruction of Women's Early Christian History," in *Searching the Scriptures*, ed. Elisabeth Schussler Fiorenza, (New York: Crossroad Publishing Company, 1993), 292.

81 Karen Jo Torjesen, "Reconstruction of Women's Early Christian History," 291.

82 M. Stephen, *New Trends in Christian Theology*, (New Delhi: Serial Publications, 2009), 111.

of Christianity as 'his-story' excluding 'her-story and experiences.[83] History should be inclusive of the works and activities of women too wherever they are so. The achievements of one gender group alone cannot be regarded as a fuller reflection and story and its related institutions and organisations.

### 2.1.1. Problems of History written by Mainstream Male Historians

Here I would like to highlight three possible problems which we see as problems of history written by mainstream male historians. They are avoidance of female characters in their writings, accepting prevailing cultural norms and mindset in which it was written, and use and abuse of the Bible to substantiate androcentric views.

#### *2.1.1.1. Avoidance of Female Characters*

The male historians in their writings either avoided or gave only passing remarks to female characters. This can be seen right from the biblical writings. According to Phyllis Bird, the Bible is a male's book written by male from a male dominated society. Hence, it contains a male bias where women appear mostly as adjuncts of men. This is the reason for the dominance of male imagery, male languages and symbols in the Bible.[84]

Even though women played important roles both in the Bible times and early church histories, many of their activities are excluded. For instance, the unnamed slave girl in the OT historical books (II Kings 5), the unnamed, brave and devout women in the early church history such as Blandina, the mystic and prophet who willingly embraced martyrdom by publicly professing her faith; the two women catechumens Perpetua and Felicity who were martyred by being forced to battle with wild beasts.[85] Another example is of Joan of Arc and Catherine of Sienna who were the main figures for the transfer of the Papacy from Avignon to Rome. But credit was

83 R. L. Hnuni, *Vision for Women in India*, (Bangalore: Asian Trading Corporation, 2009), 31.

84 R. L. Hnuni, *Vision for Women in India*, 32.

85 Anula Irvin Suguna, "The Role of Women in Evangelization," 18.

given to Pope Gregory by historians. Many who wrote history of the medieval period did not record Catherine's contributions. Even women writers ignored women and the roles they played in history.[86] Margaret Deansley who wrote history of the Middle Ages did not mention Catherine's name even though she played an important role in that period of church history.[87]

Even the Pentecostal historians from Kerala did not record of many women pioneers' significant contributions. Even when they are mentioned it was merely a passing reference in relation to men's role. For example, the Indian Christian women workers such as Ponnamma Sanyasini, Annama Mammen and many others who left a great impression gave great contribution through their evangelistic activities and their heart touching songs are not projected in writings. The above references provide us a vivid picture of the women in the history of Christianity.

Among Protestants, a few women played prominent roles in the modern missionary movement, far more prominent roles than they would have played in their own countries. Not only as wives of missionaries, but also some of them led entire mission societies and worked for the emancipation of women.

Women have always been the backbone of the many missionary endeavours. Often the lists of names are overlooked or dismissed their names as of little interest or importance.[88] Such ignored lists that provide personal, historical and social details will be helpful in understanding or applying the real situation behind the growth of church and how they exercised some kind of leadership role. Without their involvement Christianity would not have become what it is today.[89]

In the light of such neglect, the history of Christianity must be rewritten to bring back into limelight the lives of many dedicated and committed women who suffered and were martyred for God's Kingdom and many who have worked for the growth of

86 R. L. Hnuni, *Vision for Women in India*, 32.

87 V. V. Thomas, "Contribution of Women to the Indian Church," 182.

88 David M. Scholer, "Paul's Women Co-workers in Ministry," *Daughters of Sarah*, Vol. 6, no.4, 1980, 99.

89 David M. Scholr, "Paul's Women Co-workers in Ministry," 99.

Christianity. Then only we will be able to view history of the church as a comprehensive and factual account.

The researcher has noted the lack of Pentecostal literature that advocates women in ministry. Since my focus has been on the impact of Pentecostal women in Kerala on the affirmation of women ministers in the Pentecostal movement, in my research, throughout my reading I have come across numerous examples of women who persevered in ministry within a system that included specific boundaries for their ministry. Though, many women's active ministry has touched the lives of thousands, yet some of the documents related to the history of the Pentecostal movement, has not given enough space to their status and role. In short, women with leadership roles in the church have often failed to find its place on the printed page.[90]

There are also some examples of male historians who did not do any better or fair dealing and justice to the female characters, one of them which is familiar among the Pentecostals in Kerala is the 'History of Kerala Pentecostalism' (K. E. Abraham's book) written by Saju.[91] One of the main problems clearly seen in Saju's work is that, though he had recorded documents in a few pages related to the involvement of women in mission, yet gender bias is seen in the pages of 'History of Kerala Pentecostalism.' In this book the author, for instance gives an almost whole section to the activities of its male leaders but scarcely mentions the participation of women missionaries and their contributions. He ignores the major involvement and contribution of women in the Pentecostal history in Kerala (church). It is to be noted that author refers the women characters only in passive way, regrettably their lives and work have been considered secondary to that of men within this book. Perhaps the cultural norms may be one of the possibilities that the contribution of women is left out of the historical records. However, from my research, it is evident that women too were actively and significantly involved in the emergence and establishment of the Pentecostal movement in Kerala. Many "called and anointed" women served as pastors, missionaries, evangelists, church planters, founders of churches. It is

---

90 Barbara L. Cavaness, "Leadership Attitudes and the Ministry of Single Women in Assemblies of God Missions," 112.

91 Saju, *Kerala Penthekosthu Charithram*, 222-231.

also true that many of their male associates in ministry treated them as "co-labourers" and sought their counsel.

In answer to how the Pentecostal message was carried so far so fast, Harvey Cox advances two crucial factors, the first of which is women in ministry leadership. The main factor is the extraordinary part that women have played in the spread of the movement. Pentecostalism is unthinkable without women. Seymour was touched in his youth by a woman with a gift, and then recommended by a second woman to a third who actually provided him with a place to exercise his call. From Sister Hutchins and Aimee Semple McPherson to Kathryn Kuhlman, women have continued to play a disproportionately prominent place in the Pentecostal movement.[92]

The beginning of Pentecostal movement in Kerala was almost similar to what Harvey Cox mentioned. But it is so unfortunate to say that some of the women with leadership roles in the church failed to find their place in the annals. For example, there are many women missionaries (native & foreign) influenced many male leaders within the early years of ministry in Kerala, especially before the establishment of AG church in Kerala.[93] Therefore, the researcher here argues that women in this book 'History of Kerala Pentecostalism' known as 'Kerala Penthecosthu Charithram' were not passive rather active. They were active as preachers, singers, writers, poets and evangelists who visited a number of places, and were also instrumental in the foundation of many churches in Kerala.

The above mentioned examples draw to a conclusion that women were either silenced or ignored within the pages of history of Christianity. This gives us a picture of the domination of men over women in historiography which is challenged by the feminists. This kind of approach to history can only give a distorted and one sided interpretation of history. Hence, a broad shift in historiography is necessary for telling the story of women for digging out the smallest

92 Harvey Cox, *Fire from Heaven: The Rise of Pentecostal Spirituality and the Reshaping of Religion in the Twenty-first Century*, 131. See also Barbara Cavaness, "Leadership Attitudes and the Ministry of Single Women in Assemblies of God Missions," 113.

93 Finny George, "Keralathile Assemblies of Godnte Ulbhavaum Valarchayum" (The origin and growth of Assemblies of God), *Doothan*, (February, 1995): 8.

details of a time or place- history from the bottom up, instead of a history from the top down.[94] There are neglected areas and ignored characters that need to be taken up in our study of history.

In order to recover the distorted and biased history, the Pentecostal women historians have started writing about their experience, struggles and vision. In recent years, there also arose many feminist theologians/writers from various Evangelical Protestant churches who through their pen silenced the male critics. Therefore, as a woman researcher, I assert that history needs to be re-visited and rewritten.

### *2.1.1.2. Accepting Prevailing Cultural Norms and Religious Mindset*

There are cultural norms as well as religious mindsets supporting the notion that women are not equipped to assume leadership roles in the church. The prevailing attitudes, social conditions and council decisions are used to subdue and control the status and roles of women.[95] This type of traditional mind set is very much evident from Jesus' time. Most Jewish and Greek men, if not all, had negative views about women, but Jesus treated women with dignity and respect which can be seen in the gospel narratives. Women had no provision for study in the time of Jesus. But Jesus included them in His teaching illustrations, making it clear that His message involved them. Jesus viewed them not in terms of their sex, but in terms of their relationship to God.[96] Thus by honouring them He put women at par with men, demanding the same standard from both the sexes and offering the same way of salvation.

Throughout the historical narrative both men and women contributed immensely. However, due to patriarchal hegemony and male being the author highlighted the role of women only if it is needed. The splendid examples to be located as mentioned earlier are

---

94 Barbara L. Cavaness, "Leadership Attitudes and the Ministry of Single women in Assemblies of God missions," 112.

95 James B. Hurley, *Man and Woman in Biblical Perspective*, (Grand Rapids: Zondervan Publishing House, 2001), 64.

96 Richard Bauckham, *Gospel Women: Studies of the Name Women in the Gospel*, (Michigan: Wm B. Eerdmans Publishing Company, 2002), 121.

the role of unknown slave woman in II Kings. The narrator in the story projects Naaman and the powerful Elisha. A closer reading of the text shows the role of the slave woman/ girl who played a pivotal role in creating a space to reveal God's powerful arm. There are many other references where women played greater roles (Midwives, Miriam, Jochebed in Exodus narrative; Deborah in the book of Judges and also Ruth and Esther). The role of women is also seen in N.T. For example in John's Gospel, women played a very important role in the mission and ministry of Jesus (Mary in Jn 2 [Jesus' public ministry]; Mary in Jn 13 [Preparing Jesus' burial] and Mary in Jn 20 [Post-resurrection event]). In the origin and growth of Christianity, the women's role are ignored or silenced due to the cultural norms prevailed in the first century. The 12 disciples were chosen by Jesus keeping in mind the norms of that time, but there are ample references to show that women also contributed in the mission of Jesus though not recognized in par with 'the twelve disciples.'

The above references clearly indicate that from the very beginning of the church women played a significant role in its service and ministry; and from the beginning that role was challenged from various people for different reasons. Even today, there are debates within the Christian church over the full inclusion of women in the church ministries.

### *2.1.1.3. Use and Abuse of the Bible*

The main stream historians use the Bible as the base to substantiate the superiority of male over female. There are mainly two reasons behind the use and misuse of the Bible.

Firstly, in the Gospels the majority of disciples named are men. They were the products of a culture which strongly emphasized the superiority of men and the subordination of women.[97]

Secondly, those writings within a Jewish milieu were affected by the dictum of second temple Judaism in the Inter-testamental period that women could not study Torah. Since, the Gospels present Jesus as a Rabbi at least during the earlier part of his ministry, it would have been quite difficult for the Jewish evangelists to portray women

97 Jean Damilelon, *The Ministry of Women in the Early Church*, (London: The Failt Press, 1961), 115.

as rabbinic disciples receiving instruction from their teacher on an equal basis with men disciples. But in the radical newness of Jesus' servant mode of discipleship women also could learn from him, follow him, serve and be his disciples.[98]

The Bible does not speak about gender distinction in the field of ministry. God used both men and women as leaders of people even in the strictest of patriarchal societies. God showed that he valued women leaders. During the period of the itinerant Galilean ministry there may also have been a problem with contemporary social convention. In the first century it was not socially acceptable for women to wander about the countryside following a male teacher and camping in the open in proximity to a group of men. It was precisely this practice of Jesus in the open and not just in the Synagogue that enabled women to be his disciples. If, he had confined His teaching to synagogue and temple, women would have been barred altogether from listening to him. The evangelists knowing the situation of the time seem to have attempted to resolve the problem by acknowledging the presences of women who followed Jesus, but at the same time keeping these women in the background as much as possible. In spite of all these cultural and religious reasons, the evangelists did portray women following Jesus throughout His earthly ministry. Women disciples of Jesus though not at par with the 12 recognised disciples are found in all four gospels. Only the shape and extent of the role of these women were qualified by each the Gospel individual evangelist according to his own theological biases.[99] Elisabeth S. Fiorenza may be quite correct in her suggestion, 'It is probable that the gospel redactors were intentionally seeking to minimize the discipleship and apostolic activity of women, even to the extent of altering the tradition they had received.'[100]

Elisabeth Fiorenza suggests that the biblical history and stories are written and interpreted from masculine point of views. They are presented as an objective representation of what really happened.

---

98 Jean Damilelon, *The Ministry of Women in the Early Church*, 115.

99 Jean Damileon, *The Ministry of Women in the Early Church*, 116.

100 Elisabeth Schüssler Fiorenza, "Missionaries, Apostles, Co-workers: Romans 16 and the Construction of Women's Early Christian History", in *Feminist Theology: A Reader*, ed. Ann Loades, (Great Britain: SPCK 1990), 70.

One of the examples she illustrates from Paul's letters is especially striking where Apostle Paul on one hand knows women who perform duties and functions within the early Christian communities, while on the other hand, Luke, in the Acts of the Apostles, conveys the impression that the beginnings and development of the church were purely the work of men. Schussler Fiorenza therefore emphasizes that the biblical texts themselves are not exempt from the suspicion of androcentrism. The Bible was written by men; consequently, it reflects their view of reality.[101]

Since it was a patriarchal world and that the Biblical writers were males operating from a male centred world view, feminist Biblical writers are rediscovering that in the Bible women played much more significant role than what is actually recorded for us in the Bible.

### 2.1.2. Rectifications of the Problems of Mainstream Male Centred Historiography

The history of Christianity was constructed out of early traditions, which took shape in the patriarchal milieu of the Mediterranean society. Thus, the literary legacy of the first generation of Christians is distorted by the cultural assumption that male activity is normative. Elisabeth Fiorenza, in her book *In Memory of Her* provides a critical analysis of the way androcentric selection of traditions and translations have suppressed the memory of women's contribution to formative Christianity.[102] The androcentrism of ancient Mediterranean societies compartmentalized the area into two spheres- the sphere of private and sphere of public. In ancient culture public sphere of the state was superior to the private sphere. Public life is referred to male identity and private life referred to the domestic sphere which was the locus of female identity. The gender ideology that described the *polis* (city) as a male domain and

---

101 Monica Fander, "Historical-Critical Methods: Searching the Scriptures," in *A Feminist Introduction,* (ed.), Elisabeth Schüssler Fiorenza, Vol. 1 (New York: The Crossroad Publishing Company, 1993), 215, 216.

102 Elisabeth Schüssler Fiorenza, *In Memory of Her: A Feminist Theological Reconstruction of Christian Origins*, (New York: Crossroad, 1983), 41-61.

the *oikos* (household) as a female sphere segregating women from public, political life and giving them roles in the private sphere.[103]

The public-private gender ideology was supported by a system of cultural values that differentiated between male and female honour. Since, Christian writers viewed women's activities through the lens of their society's beliefs about gender, their accounts of women's activities and their practice against women's leaders must be interpreted critically in the light of the system of sexual politics in the ancient Mediterranean. As a result, women's words, achievements and their contributions to formative Christianity have been largely suppressed or ignored. Although, women such as Mary Magdalene were prominent in an early tradition, their importance was muted due to their beliefs about gender.[104] The various ministries of the church became institutionalized and the context of Christian worship shifted from house–churches to a more public space, the role of women leaders became increasingly controversial. Consequently, many books containing women's apostolic activity, words of women prophets, transmission of women's teachings which had nurtured the religious life of many churches, were not included in the canon, which was recognized on the basis of male authorship.[105]

Elisabeth Fiorenza says that only through a "hermeneutic of suspicion" can the actual contributions of women be discerned behind the gender rhetoric of male writers. Furthermore, she shows that women made considerable contributions to the development of Christianity during the first four centuries and provided leadership for the Christian communities throughout the Mediterranean.[106]

The theological foundations for women's leadership were laid in the Christian vision of the reign of God (*basileia*) in which God's wholeness was extended to all, making women and men equal. The androcentric retelling of women's stories, treatises from his formative period reveal that women were apostles, prophets, and teachers; that they exercised a diversity of ministries including baptizing,

---

103 Karen Jo Torjesen, *Reconstruction of Women's Early Christian History*, 290.

104 Karen Jo Torjesen, *Reconstruction of Women's Early Christian History*, 291.

105 Karen Jo Torjesen, *Reconstruction of Women's Early Christian History*, 291.

106 Elisabeth Schüssler Fiorenza, *In Memory of Her*, 109.

disciplining and presiding over the Eucharist; also in church offices as bishop, presbyter, widow, deacon, and virgin.[107]

### *2.1.2.1. Give Space and Voice to the Women Characters and the Roles they Played*

To address this I would like to investigate briefly about the role of women in the earliest church, the roles women played in leadership, and in church activities and what restrictions and opposition women faced during this period.

#### *2.1.2.1.1. Women Partners in God's Mission*

In the New Testament era women became increasingly prominent. According to A. T. Pierson, 'a marked feature of the New Acts of the apostle is the apostle of women from the day when Gabriel announced to the Virgin Mary.'[108] Woman had taken a new rank in history since then. Anna, the first woman missionary in NT, who prophesied regarding the new born Messiah, the woman of Samaria who led the whole village towards Christ; and also Mary of Bethany, caring women (Luke 8:2-3), daughters of Jerusalem (Luke 22:27) are all powerful examples of women being partners in God's mission along with men.

#### *2.1.2.1.2. Women as Ministers to Jesus*

Jesus ministered to men but the women ministered to Him. Although, *Diakoneo* may be used in an official sense of serving as deacons or in a general sense of attending to anything, especially the supplying of necessities of life, it is used in general sense of the women who ministered to Jesus in the Gospels. Martha waited on the table; Jesus received money from wealthy women (Lk. 8:2-3). Women were honoured to tell others, about the news of the resurrection first, simply because they were being faithful to their duties. They were present at the tomb that first Easter morning, and they brought

107 Elisabeth Schüssler Fiorenza, *In Memory of Her*, 140-150.

108 Sakhi Athyal cites A. T. Peirson, "Women and Men together as God's Agents of Transformation", *Journal of Theological Education and Mission,* Vol. 5, (2014): 41.

spices for Jesus' body and were caring for the physical need in the time of death.[109]

### *2.1.2.1.3. Women of the Early Church*

The book of Acts and Epistles portrays a number of devout and honourable women who played the important role in the ministry of the early church. On the day of Pentecost, women spoke in tongues (Acts 2:1-4). According to the scriptures, the preaching of the gospel after Pentecost was done not only by the apostles, but also by scattered church members, manifestly inclusive of both sexes.[110] Many of these women were persecuted by Saul of Tarsus and suffered much for their faith.[111] On a number of occasions, women's home was the meeting place for the church. The importance of women in the early Christian beginnings is shunned, greatly owing to the 'andro-centric historiography.'[112] However, it is clear that the early church was a movement of both men and women. Mary, Rhoda, Tabitha, Pricilla, Lydia, Euodia, Syntyche, Damarius, Phoebe, Junia, Tryphane, Tryphose, etc., had important roles in the life and ministry of the early church. Some of these women were very significant. In the early church, women played an important role as prophetesses. The daughters of Philip, the Evangelist were prophetesses.[113]

### ***2.1.2.2. Recognize Women's Constituency within the Church (Numerical Strength)***

In order to understand women's role in Christian tradition we need to identify two realities in the context within which the history of Christianity has been written until very recently. The first reality is that when we study the history of Christianity we can affirm that at least half of the Christians who have lived since the movement begun in the first century A.D. have been women. From the very beginning

109 Sakhi Athyal, "Women and Men Together as God's Agents," 40.

110 L. E. Maxwell, *Women in Ministry,* (England: Victor Books, 1987), 18-30.

111 Sakhi Athyal, "Women and Men Together as God's Agents," 41.

112 Ruth A. Tucker and Walter L. Liefield, *Daughters of the Church: Women and Ministry from NT Times to the Present,* 33.

113 K. J. Mathew, "Women in Church and Society," 19.

of the church women played an important role and their contribution has been well recognized.[114] In many instances women had crucial leadership roles in the growth and development of the church. Yet, the church historians have limited their roles in not writing a detailed account but selected a few fractions of materials and re-wrote what was necessary for their theological argument from a patriarchal point of view.[115] Even today, although women formed the majority of membership in the church, yet, they were not given place in the administration of the church or in the leadership positions. They are still in the clutches of men's world. It is interesting to note that most of the churches in principle accept the equality of women in the sight of God. The unfortunate side is that this understanding is not turned into attitude of action. As a result the structure of patriarchy plays a dominant role and their voices are always controlled by the church leaders.[116]

The second and equally challenging reality is that historians of Christianity have largely ignored the role played by this half of the church. Unfortunately, the sources of information for this phase are scarce and often fragmentary and ambiguous.[117] It is true that the role/s of women is not mentioned because the historians were men, and men who did not attach any importance to the role of women. In fact the vast majority of published church histories are written by men.[118] The sources seldom mention about women and refer to them only in passing remarks. Even these few documents were generally recorded by males and display a male preconception. Even those sources written by women were preserved by a male cultural system. These are the limitations we need to keep in mind.[119]

---

114 V. V. Thomas, "Contribution of Women to the Indian Church," 174.

115 Charles Caldwell Ryrie, *The Role of Women in the Church*, (Chicago: Moody Press, 1970), 16-57.

116 M. Stephen, *Towards a Pentecostal Theology and Ethics*, 50 and V. V. Thomas, "Contribution of Women to the Indian Church," 174, 178.

117 P. Karunanidhi, "The Situation of Women in the Early Period," *History of Christianity*, 1.

118 Roger Gryson, *The Ministry of Women in the Early Church*, trans. Jean Laporate and Mary Louise Hall, (Minnesota: The Liturgical Press, 1976), 11-43.

119 P. Karunanidhi, "The Situation of Women in the Early Period," 8.

### *2.1.2.3. Recognize the Space given to Women in the Bible though they are Scanty*

The Bible, in fact, contains a rich record of women who were placed in authority by God. Jesus Christ's first coming was revolutionary for all, but especially for women who were for the most part excluded from Jewish ritual. Baptism was open to everyone, as was the call to share the good news. The Samaritan woman at the well was perhaps the first female missionary to bring a town to Christ. The first to be given the mission of spreading the news of the resurrection was a woman named Mary. And, on the day of Pentecost, traditionally celebrated only by Jewish males, both men and women received the outpouring of the Holy Spirit and were enabled to speak with prophetic authority in the church (Acts 1 and 2). Peter's message from Joel 2:28-29, that "sons and daughters" would prophecy, has since been the anchor for many women in ministry, particular for those with roots in the holiness movement of the nineteenth century.[120]

The Gospel writers explicitly mention the presence of women among the disciples by their name. These women were not just spectators who stayed at the back of Jesus' entourage watching Him from a distance. They were Jesus' disciples in the fullest sense, and we have every reason to believe that women disciples of Jesus are found in all four gospels. The shape and extend of the role of these women were qualified by each individual evangelist according to his own theological bias. They were tended to minimize the role of women from their theological point of view.[121]

There are several other examples of women who held positions of spiritual authority in the New Testament church. Like Jesus, Apostle Paul had women disciples whom he trained and commissioned to preach and evangelise on the front lines. Around thirteen women who are known by name have been leaders in the Pauline churches. Paul, in his letters, named 54 men within the churches, presumably all of whom had some leadership role. This means that nearly twenty percent of Paul's co-workers were

120 Barbara Cavaness, "God Calling: Women in Assemblies of God Missions," *Pneuma, The Journal of the Society for Pentecostal Studies,* Vol. 16, (1994): 50.

121 Jean Damilelon, *The Ministry of Women in the Early Church,* 115.

women! When the issues of Paul's view of women in the church are addressed, these women co-workers in the ministry must not be forgotten. They are crucial, determinative evidence for the overall assessment of Paul's view. Therefore, it would not be an overstatement to say that women played the role of change and they actually exercised authority and leadership as a natural part among the people of God.[122]

### 2.1.3. Reconstruct History with Specific Focus on Women

The reconstruction of women's role in the beginning of Christianity depends on two kinds of sources, literary and documentary. Both were formed in the patriarchal cultural milieu of the ancient Mediterranean. On the one hand, the literary sources speak in terms of woman functions to minimize woman's power, etc., whereas, on the other hand, documentary sources explain women's activities and to portraits function to enhance the honour of a family through highlighting the achievements of an individual woman.[123]

Bernadette Brooten has demonstrated the importance of documentary sources for reconstructing the history of women in Judaism. By studying Jewish inscriptions, she demonstrates that Jewish women held important offices, including ruler of the synagogue, elder, priest and mother of the synagogue.[124] Through this documentary evidence it is striking to know how widespread women's leadership in Jewish communities was until six centuries. The preliminary studies of documentary evidence present a similar picture of women's leadership and Christian women who were presbyters in their congregations.[125] Evidence for women holding the office of deacon is equally impressive. During the first three centuries the office of deacon was functioned by both men and women. By the

122 David M. Scholer, "Paul's Women Co-workers in Ministry," 99.

123 Karen Jo Torjesen, *Reconstruction of Women's Early Christian History*, 292.

124 Bernadette Brooten, *Women Leaders in the Ancient Synagogue*, (Chico, CA: Scholars Press, 1982).

125 Karen Jo Torjesen, *Reconstruction of Women's Early Christian History*, 293.

fourth century the office of deaconess appears as a woman's office whose ministry was exclusively to women.[126]

In Rome, the most important college was made up of priestesses of Vesta whose residence was situated at the administrative heart of the Roman Empire. These women priests enjoyed some of the rights and privileges of male magistrates.[127] Women's extensive participation in both Greek and Roman religious rites reveals that neither of these societies considered women's gender an impediment to religious leadership.[128] These are the evidences from Christian literary sources to support the evidence of the documentary sources that women participated in a wide variety of ministries and were recognized as leaders in their local congregations. Although, women held the familiar church offices of bishop, presbyter, and deacon, these sources do not record the actual functions of these women, however, the literary sources gives an accounts of women's ministries.[129]

These are the documentary and literary sources that provide evidences to support us to reconstruct history with specific focus on women's leadership throughout this period and into the succeeding centuries.

According to Fiorenza, "women were the first non-Jews to become members of the Jesus' movement."[130] Referring to the Galilean women she further says that 'they were not very decisive for the extension of the Jesus movement to gentiles but also for the very continuation of this movement after Jesus' arrest and execution.'[131] They did not flee after his arrest but stayed in Jerusalem for His execution and burial. They were the first to articulate the powerful goodness of God in raising Jesus from the dead. Added to this there are many other roles played by the women in Jesus movement which makes it obvious that the discipleship of women is the reconstruction

126 Bernadette Brooten, "Early Christian Women and Their Cultural Context," in *Feminist Perspectives on Biblical Scholarship*, ed. Adela Yarbro Collins, (Chico, CA: Scholars Press, 1985), 65-92.

127 Karen Jo Torjesen, *Reconstruction of Women's Early Christian History*, 295.

128 Dorothy Irvin, *The Ministry of Women in the Early Church*, 77-78.

129 Karen Jo Torjesen, *Reconstruction of Women's Early Christian History*, 295.

130 Elisabeth Schüssler Fiorenza, *In Memory of Her*, 135.

131 Elisabeth Schüssler Fiorenza, *In Memory of Her*, 135.

of the events after the death and resurrection of Jesus is plausible, and by continuing to keep alive the good news about the manifestation of God's life-giving power in Jesus of Nazareth, among the followers and friends of Jesus, the Galilean women continued the movement initiated by Jesus.[132]

As we have noted, the early Christian movement or the so-called Jesus movement was inclusive of women's leadership and so can be called 'egalitarian.'[133] Fiorenza reminds us that our sources of information mainly the book of Acts and the epistles of the New Testament along with scattered later material on church order have been written and interpreted in patriarchal cultures with unfortunate results. She urges us to remember that what we know about the activities of women probably only represents the tip of the iceberg. Therefore it is likely that women participated in the early development of the church to a much greater extent than our sources imply.[134]

Women were the active members of Christian communities. They are considered as the tip of an iceberg in which the most prominent women of the early Christian movement missionary surface, not as exceptions to the rule but as representatives of early Christian women who have survived androcentric redactions and historical silence.[135] Such a reconstruction of the Christian missionary movement in which the women member as missionary agents on the one hand and the home churches and the local associations on the other, in terms of organisational structures provides the social frame work that makes women's leadership not only plausible but also intelligible.

The investigation of the theological implication of the historical reconstruction of Jesus movement and early church reveal that the role and participation of women in both is plausible but sadly they were overshadowed by the dominant patriarchal system. Hence, the historical reconstruction of Jesus movement and early church is to look at these personal attitudes more clearly and systematically

132 Bernadette Brooten, "Early Christian Women," 80.

133 Elisabeth Schüssler Fiorenza, *In Memory of Her*, 141.

134 Elisabeth Schüssler Fiorenza, *In Memory of Her*, 141.

135 Elisabeth Schüssler Fiorenza, *In Memory of Her*, 168.

reconstruct a Jesus movement not as his-story or her-story but as 'Human story.'

Based on the evidence from the scripture, first century church and from the early history of the church it is possible to assert that there were women ministers if not apostles in the primitive church, and He commissioned them to minister in His name. Over the centuries male commentators have sought to obscure this fact, since it would threaten the presupposition that the official ministry of the church was from the beginning reserved to men. Perhaps many more women, besides the ones referred walk through the pages of the New Testament writings. Hence, it is clear that the early church was a movement of both men and women.

## 2.2. The Place and Role of Women in the History of Christianity

In this section, I will be exploring place and the role of women in the history of Christianity in the world and the place and role of women in the history of Christianity in India.

### 2.2.1. The Place and Role of Women in the History of Christianity in the World

Throughout the early church history especially in the second and third centuries, we have many instances of virgins and widows who played important roles in the ministry of the early church.[136] In the third century initially there was a male movement called monasticism and it was much more of a lay than a clerical movement. Hilda was the Abbess in what are called "double monasteries" that is, monasteries in which women and men were domiciled, although different quarters.[137] Later there also began monastic groups for women and they were the nuns. Their ministries was fast and pray for the sick and the distressed church members, visiting them and what is most remarkable, laying hands upon them. Moreover, their mission was

---

136 Anula Irvin Suguna, "The Role of Women in Evangelisation," 18.

137 Susan E. Smith, *Women in Mission: From the New Testament to Today*, (New York: Orbis Books, 2007), 83.

anointing of women with oil after baptism, to instruct the newly baptised women, etc.[138]

In the fourth century, Christian women of high rank chose to follow an ascetical, chaste life style and minister to the poor. Marcella, a friend of Jerome in the late fourth century, is credited with being the first woman to organize such a group in her own home. There were both male and female monasteries; the latter were often called convents to distinguish from the male counterpart. From sixth to the ninth century, a number of important Benedictine nuns emerged. They 'went out' to minister among those who had not yet heard the good news, to serve the poor, the sick, and the suffering. Famous among them was the work of the poor Clares, founded by the Lady Clare of Assisi, whose ministry continues to the present day as the Second Order of St. Francis. Such monasteries were usually presided over by an Abbess among them. Hilda the Abbess was so great that not only ordinary people but even kings and princess sought and received her advice. Leoba was a co-worker of Boniface in the mission to Germanic tribes.[139]

In the late Middle Ages both men and women embraced the *vita apostolic*, the practice of voluntary poverty modelled on the example of Jesus and His first disciples claimed the right to preach. This was the third Order or Tertiaries for women seeking to pursue a mission focussed life. Some prominent tertiaries include Catherine of Siena, (was one of the most remarkable spiritual mystics of the late Middle Ages. Catherine's visions and inspirations made her to understand her duty to reform the church, to evangelize, to comfort the sick, the poor and the condemned. She was an activist in an age when a women's religious vocation was supposed to be confined and apart from the world), Margaret of Cortona and many others. It was a time of extraordinary growth of women religious communities, both contemplative and active. These women appear as mystics, theologians, great administrators, managers and as courageous missionaries who served and ministered to the poor, the sick and the

138 P. Karunanidhi, "The Situation of Women in the Early Period," 3-4.

139 Susan E. Smith, *Women in Mission: From the New Testament to Today*, 18; Georgia Harkness, *A Historical and Theological Inquiry*, (Nashville: Abingdon Press, 1972), 80-81.

outcasts. In the sixteenth century, we could see St. Teresa of Avila who was a mystic. She was a remarkable woman, not only in the depth of her spiritual insights but in her tireless labours for the spiritual life of the church. The middle centuries gave women a status and opportunity for personhood not available elsewhere in the history. The vows of poverty, chastity, and obedience, illumined with a sense of religious calling in their life.[140]

In the seventeenth century women seized the opportunity to step out as missionaries. The contributions that women made to Catholic missions are tremendous. Among them are Teresa of Avila, Angela Merci, Mary Ward, Jeanne de Chantal, Louise de Marillac, Ursuline Marie Guyart and Marguerite Bourgeys. The fact that they were deeply spiritual, courageous and prophetic women enabled them to respond with faith and hope to the changing world.[141] In almost same period some Baptist and Quaker women, less ecclesiastically trammelled began to preach, but in general the restriction on the preaching or other public ministry of women continued. Quakers obviously demonstrated equality to women. George Fox, the founder of this movement strongly defended the full involvement of women in ministry. However, Tucker observes that in later periods, there was opposition to the active role of women in the church and Quaker women never enjoyed complete equal status.[142]

In Methodism and in the Holiness movement which is its offshoot, women and their various ministries were recognized. Phoebe Palmer and Nelly Terry were mighty preachers of this movement. One of the leaders of the Welsh revival (1904) was Florae Evans, a young girl.[143] Some strong women emerged during this period, both Queens and house wives. Susannah Wesley is an example of the latter who has made a place for herself in history, a woman of remarkable ability and well educated for her time. There were other women of

140 Georgia Harkness, *A Historical and Theological Inquiry,* 82; John D. Woodbridge, *Great Leaders of the Christian Church*, (Chicago: Moody Press, 1988), 178, 253.

141 Anula Irvin Suguna, "The Role of Women in Evangelisation," 18-19.

142 Ruth A. Tucker and Walter L. Liefield, *Daughters of the Church: Women and Ministry from NT Times to the Present*, 33.

143 Charles Caldwell Ryrie, *The Role of Women in the Church*, 10-13.

distinction, both before and after Susannah Wesley, who have left their mark on history. There was Anne Hutchinson, independent spirit in the midst of New England Calvinism, who disliked its theological rigidity and advocated a covenant of grace instead of works, with a direct approach to God through the Holy Spirit rather than the ecclesiastical authorities. Almost two centuries later, Elizabeth Fry an English Quaker minister, dared to visit unruly female prisoners and devised a scheme for giving them practical help. Her inspiration for the work was the Quaker conviction that all human beings, even the most degraded, should be treated with respect.[144]

Toward the end of eighteenth century, we find some remarkable words by a remarkable woman, Abigail Adams, the wife of the second president of the United States. In 1777 she penned this epistle:

> "In the new code of laws which I suppose it will be necessary for you to make, I desire you would remember the ladies and be more generous and favourable to them than your ancestors......... If particular care and attention is not paid to the ladies, we are determined to foment a rebellion, and will not hold ourselves bound by any laws in which we have no voice and representation."[145]

The situation began to change further from the 19th century. The nineteenth century witnessed a significant growth in Catholic missionary activity, a growth in which women played a significant role. Women missionaries responded to the needs of the poor radically. There were number of women organisation such as Sisters of Mercy, Sisters of St. Joseph of the Sacred Heart and Missionaries Sisters of Charity came forward to extend their help in different ways.[146]

144 Georgia Harkness, *A Historical and Theological Inquiry*, 83-85.

145 Georgia Harkness, *A Historical and Theological Inquiry*, 86-87.

146 Susan E. Smith, *Women in Mission: From the New Testament to Today*, 19.

### 2.2.2. The Place and Role of Women in the History of Christianity in India

The history of Christianity often portrays that the social transformation whether in secular or spiritual realm (world) is attributed as the work of men. The problem with such interpretation is that one part of the fact for social transformation is totally ignored and therefore history remains incomplete. In the light of such incomplete history, feminist historiography has come into the forefront and there is a flood of feminist literature in India today. Women's exclusion experience has forced the attention of feminist critic on history. The age long silencing of women has given way to women's voice today. It may be said here that though enormous number of feminist history and literature is available in India today, history of Christianity in India has not taken adequate steps to include women within the studies of Indian Church History. This does not mean that nothing is done at all. Recent years, secular feminist historians like Uma Chakraborty and Gauri Viswanathan and many other Christian women have written on Pandita Ramabai and conversion movements in India that includes women.[147]

The Indian church witnessed a great breakthrough with the arrival of British East India Company which made a great impact in the Indian church history. It happened mainly due to the efforts of people like William Carey and broad minded evangelicals within the British Government. A number of efforts were undertaken in the upliftment of women in the Indian society beginning from the 19$^{th}$ century. It has to be said here that Christianity and the education it brought played a great role in the development of women's place in the church history. As said earlier, even though women played crucial role in the history of Indian church, they were not given any recognition in the church, either in the internal matters of the church or in its external affairs. Mostly men handled it all.[148] Ruth A. Tucker is right in pointing out that, women, minorities, and non-westerners are often ignored in the pages of church history. She points out that

---

147 Georgia Harkness, *A Historical and Theological Inquiry,* 81-82.

148 V. V. Thomas, "Contribution of Women to the Indian Church: A Perspective from the Pentecostal Churches in India," 170-171.

"A history that focuses on those with prestige and position is not the fullest reflection of our heritage- in that it is out of step with how God works in the world."[149] A group of non-westerners also has stated that "women had played a vital role in the missionary expansion of the church; it is as large as and possibly larger than that of men, but this has not been adequately reflected in mission history."[150] From the mission work of Boniface's nun in the eighth century to the Moravian women of the eighteenth century, women have responded to God's call as agents of missions- though few of their exploits are known.[151]

Protestant spiritual awakening brought the principle of the priesthood of the believers into actual practice. Women had a growing place and laymen had more and more initiative and participation. With the arrival of the Protestant missionaries, the Indian women got some upliftment mainly because the Protestant missionaries who came brought their wives along with them and they tried to uplift the Indian women from their degraded position to the place of honour and respect. The protestant missionaries through their emphasis on education and equality of all in the sight of God brought great changes in the lives of Indian women. Mrs. Marshman established a first day school for girls in 1807. There were Baptist missionary ladies who started a society for the Indian women. In fact to a great extent one can say that the western missionaries have been the pioneers in the promotion of education for women in India. However, the prejudices against women continued to be the case in the Indian church although changes took place elsewhere.[152]

One can say without any fear of contradiction, for instance, that the modern protestant missionary movement could not have been sustained apart from the support given it by women's groups. The main supporters of those societies in the churches were women.

149 Ruth A. Tucker, "Colonizing Church History," *Christianity Today*, (1992): 20.

150 Godwin Tasie, 'History of Mission: Role of Women in Mission," *Missiology* 7, (1979): 94.

151 Barbara Cavaness, "God Calling: Women in assemblies of God Missions," 51. Also see R. Rierce Beaver, *American Protestant Women in World Mission*, (Grand Rapids, Michigan: Wm. B. Eerdmans Publishing Company, 1980).

152 V. V. Thomas, "Contribution of Women to the Indian Church," 172.

This is certainly something that can be legitimately studied by the historians of Christianity.[153]

When we took steps back into history we need to understand the barriers and humiliation that women faced. The church in India needs to come to terms with the fact that it has erected many barriers against a fuller and more meaningful participation of women. The walls of hostility between the genders need to be broken down and a new community built on oneness and love which we experience in our faith in Jesus Christ. The church in India needs to recognize the personhood of Jesus Christ and the fact that Christ is the representative human being for all people including Indian women.[154]

We could see sign of developments in the churches like Methodist church, Church of South India, etc. This shows that in these churches there was some improvement in the treatment towards women, and they were able to contribute to the development of the women in their churches. It is interesting to note that most of the churches in principle accept the equality of women in the sight of God. The unfortunate side is that this understanding is not turned into action. However as already mentioned, through the efforts of some active women some changes have been taking place in the recent years. Even among the Roman Catholic churches there have been changes taking place in recognizing the contribution that women can offer to the church and the society. One can think of the unparalleled contributions of Mother Theresa to the Indian Society.[155]

The place of women in Indian history has not always been one of low status. The two thousand year story of women's efforts to fully participate in the mission of evangelisation is a story to survive in a church whose leaders often had fixed ideas about women's role in mission. From the very beginning of the church women played a significant role in its service and ministry; and from the beginning that role was challenged from various peoples for different reasons. Women have always taken an active role in society and religion. But

153 P. Karunanidhi, "The Situation of Women in the Early Period," 3-4.

154 M. M. Virginia, Febella, Park and Sun Ai Lee (ed.), *We Dare to Dream, Doing Theology as Asian Women*, (New York: Orbis Books, 1989), 20.

155 V. V. Thomas, "Contribution of Women to the Indian Church," 174.

prevailing attitudes, social conditions and council decisions have all worked to subdue and control them.[156] But Bible clearly indicates that Jesus treated women with dignity and respect, He viewed them not in terms of their sex, but in terms of their relationship to God. By thus honouring them, He put women on equality with men, demanding the same standard from both the sexes and offering the same way of salvation. Women persisted, however in their efforts to be evangelisers with missionary enthusiasm.[157]

We can see the proof of the above statement. Even history demonstrates the tremendous contribution women have made in pioneering situations. Women have been willing workers in mission. In many cases they were the first to go and they founded works in many countries. Women have also been great pioneers in church planting. Others have founded Bible colleges. These women created their own positions by pioneering new works.[158]

The status and role of women throughout the centuries are a promising and challenging one but church authorities withholding from the women the office of ministry is a discouraging story. Through the study of sacred scripture, tradition, church documents and from the historical evidences we can affirm that the women have impacted change and continue to initiate and influence changes in the history of the church.

### *2.2.2.1. Women in the History of Pentecostal and Charismatic Movements in India*

The attempt here is to provide a brief history of new dimension in the ministerial life of Pentecostal women. The Pentecostals trace back their origin to the day of Pentecost (Lk. 24:19; Acts. 2). The *glossolalia* (speaking in tongues) is acknowledged by the Pentecostals as the distinctive experience along with the gift of prophecy, miracles (healing, etc) and the visions. As I mentioned in my first chapter,

156 Santhosh John, "Feminism: A Contemporary Theological Critique," *Conviction: Journal of Bethel Bible College*, 1.2 (2013): 58.

157 Santosh John, "Feminism: A Contemporary Theological Critique," 58.

158 Deborah M. Gill and Barbara Cavaness, *God's Women Then and Now, Study Guide*, (Springfield: Grace and Truth, 2007), 204.

these phenomena are also found all through the centuries. Hence, the Pentecostal experience has a long history.

The first Pentecostal experience is mentioned in the Acts of the Apostles (Jerusalem-experience Acts-2). Luke points out the possibility of the presence of women at this Pentecost. He had noted their presence in the upper room with the eleven. The sermon of Peter served to interpret the event of Pentecost for the whole people. Peter cites a passage from Joel which mentioned the pouring out of the Spirit upon "sons and daughters," "menservants and maidservants." Luke's inclusion of this quotation suggests that women were in fact present at that Pentecost. Pentecost was the event of the birth of the church. It was also the event of the empowering of the members of the Christian community for mission. Thus, it is of great theological importance whether women were present at this event as a basis for their full participation in the subsequent mission of the church. It is also significant that Luke never again mentions Mary after Acts 1:14. He gave her no role during the period of the church. This may have been a result of his theological position on the role of women in the church. It may also simply have been due to lack of historical information.[159]

As per the account of Luke, in the first Pentecost there were men and women participated meaningfully in the work of the Holy Spirit. They celebrated the advent of the Holy Spirit. It was a 'Freedom in Christ' and 'Freedom in Spirit.' These two are the key categories of Pentecostal theology. Everyone has the right to use their freedom creatively and responsibly. Therefore, the Bible very clearly indicates that the account of Pentecost was the primary basis for supporting women in ministry among Pentecostals.[160]

In studying the references to the presence of women in the day of Pentecost, it becomes evident that the manifestation of this power emphasis on the baptism of the Holy Spirit provided the basis for its affirmation of women's full participation in mission. In fact, it

---

159 Jean Damilelon, *The Ministry of Women in the Early Church*, 106, 109.

160 M. Stephen, *Towards a Pentecostal Theology and Ethics*, 51.

provides the doctrinal emphasis on a positive theological context for women in ministry.[161]

Susie C. Stanley noted that the experience of Pentecost confirmed that the baptism of the Holy Ghost provided power for Jesus' followers to spread the gospel. The power that came to the early disciples is the same that comes to us today, and comes in the same way. The story of Pentecost was the primary basis for taking sides towards women in ministry among Pentecostals. That is a great encouragement to the women today. When the Holy Spirit descended at Pentecost, there was no selection process based on gender. According to Acts 2:4, they all spoke as the Spirit gave them utterance. Does not the 'all' include the women present? Was not their speaking as the Spirit gave utterance the act of a minister in preaching? It was obvious that the answer to these questions was "yes."[162]

It is therefore possible that women were present when the disciples received the risen Jesus' solemn commission to ministry and the gift of his Holy Spirit. On the basis of this evidence, it is right to believe that when Jesus sent the Holy Spirit upon the church, as recorded in the book of Acts, many of these same women were in the upper room and received empowerment on the day of Pentecost. If so I surely believe that God does not have a preferential option for any particular gender, but the church has not been able to reconcile with this fact.[163]

The church must hear God's voice clearly on this subject of women in ministry so that it can cooperate with Him and His Great Commission. Therefore, we must never find ourselves working against His purposes, quenching His Spirit at work in those whom He had called to extend His kingdom. As we release women, we'll mobilize the hundreds of thousands of people needed to complete the great Commission. We'll see when God's blessing and more

---

161 Susie C. Stanley, "Wesleyan/Holiness and Pentecostal Women Preachers: Pentecost as the Pattern for Primitivism," in *Philip's Daughters,* ed. Estrelda Alexander and Amos Yong, (Oregon: Pickwick Publications, 2009), 28.

162 Susie C. Stanley, "Wesleyan/Holiness and Pentecostal Women Preachers: Pentecost as the Pattern for Primitivism," 35.

163 J. lee Grady, "Let the Women Preach," 57.

anointing of the spirit come upon them there will be unity within the church and will have effective leadership. We'll see throughout the centuries, God through His Spirit has attempted again and again to bring renewal and correction to His people.[164]

The study of female prophetism by Deborah Gill shows a clear connection between rejection of the charismata in the early church and the objection to women in leadership in the church. Having argued for the leadership role of prophet throughout the Biblical period and in the first century church she points out that,

> Whenever......religion was characterized more by vitality than by institutionalisation, when the qualification for leadership were more spiritual (charismatic) than professional, when divine endorsement was valued over social legitimation, i.e., when the religion was prophetic instead of priestly- that is when women were involved in religious leadership." She further says "Charismatic religious orientation is usually accompanied by openness to female leadership."[165]

According to Donald Dayton,

> "The outpouring of the Spirit on the day of Pentecost is a movement that have emphasized the role of the Holy Spirit tended to be more open to women...because in such contexts the Holy Spirit has the autonomy to call and use persons apart from normal patterns of authority." But as movements grow and mature, the "spiritual leadership of women is accepted less readily."[166]

In the light of the above observations, one can assure that on the day of Pentecost the church received the baptism of the Holy Spirit. Thereafter every individual Christians participates in this

---

164 Loren Cunningham and David Joel Hamilton, *Why Not Women?* (Seattle: YWAM Publishing, 2000), 232.

165 A. Kay fountain, "Where the Spirit of the Lord is' *Dharma Deepika,* (January-June, 2005): 33.

166 Barbara Cavaness, "God Calling: Women in Assemblies of God Missions," 61.

baptism and all are made members of the family of God. There is no evidence that the Spirit came upon men only- indeed as mentioned earlier Peter quotes Joel to show that at the coming of the Messiah all will share in the gift of the Spirit (Acts 2). Thus we see in the early church, men and women working together in the fellowship and using their gifts in God's service. Women exercise gifts of leadership. Pentecost adds therefore a new dimension to the question of ministry in the church.[167]

Therefore, 'Day of Pentecost' is not only the birth of the Christian church but also an open invitation and a direct relationship between recognition and openness to the Holy Spirit to 'all', and more than that it is a movement of releasing power and authority over women in ministry and also the amount of freedom given to women in ministry.[168] It can be also said that Pentecostalism is the segment of Christianity which believes that there is an unique aspect of the spirit's manifestation, namely baptism in the spirit and the initial physical evidence of the Spirit's baptism is speaking in tongues. They also believe that this baptism in the spirit is normative for every Christian believer irrespective of gender. They believe that the New Testament record of the event of Pentecost is not merely a "record of what happened in one generation, but a blue print of what should happen in every generation until Jesus returns again."[169]

After having a close examination of the call and role of women leaders involved in Pentecostal mission, the author wants to urge the Pentecostal churches to be more open to the Holy Spirit, to recognize the "pastorally gifted women" and to allow women to exercise their leadership role in the church.

The origin of Modern Pentecostal movement that took firm root among the Syrian Christians in Kerala can be traced back to this and similar revival and reformation movements led by numerous native revival Christian preachers like Kochu Kunjuapadesi, Panchamannil Mammen Upadesi, Justus Joseph, Mahakavai K. V.

---

167 George Carey, "Women and Authority in the Scriptures", Furlong, 48.

168 A. Kay Fountain, "Where the Spirit of the Lord is", 33.

169 David Duplessis, "Pentecost", *A Quarterly Review of World-wide Pentecost Activity*, Vol. 30, (December, 1954): 17.

Simon and many other known and unknown revival preachers and wandering charismatics (men and women) of that time.[170]

Similar revival took place among the Christian converts in Tirunelveli and Travancore in 1860s and 1870s as a result of the influence of many male and female missionaries from CMS and Pietistic background.[171] According to McGee and Burgess, this revival took an indigenous turn. Missionaries and western money had little or no influence in evangelistic outreach where men and women were involved. These revivals emerged as a protest against the nominalism beliefs and practices of the traditional Episcopal churches.[172] Through the influence of Aroolappan family and their followers, the movement spread westward a decade later in to nearby Travancore. Some of the highlights of this revival were the negation of caste, involvement of women in ministry, *glossolalia* and other related spiritual phenomena, etc.

According to one of the leading Assemblies historians, Garry B. McGee 'Towards the beginning of the 20th century', the first Pentecostal experience was manifested in the northeast of India in Khassia Hills revival broke out (in March 1905) among the tribal peoples of north east at Welsh Presbyterian mission stations and among Christian and Alliance mission's missionaries at Akola, Maharastra in 1906 but this was not documented.[173] Another Pentecostal-like revival was witnessed among the girls at the Mukti mission run by Panditha Ramabai a Brahmin convert to Christianity. This was a result of the revival of which an eye witness, Minnie F. Abrams reported that "there was weeping, long prayer, confession of sins, and visions. However, Pentecosal and Charismatic Movements in India appeared through the efforts of the Western Missionaries

170 Simon Samuel, "The Charismatic and Pentecostal Movements and their Commitments to the Social Demands of the Gospel," 224.

171 G. B. McGee and S. M. Burges, 'India,' 118.

172 M. Stephen, *Towards a Pentecostal Theology and Ethics*, 51.

173 Garry B. McGee, *Selected Documents on the Early History of the Assemblies of God in India*, (Spring Field, 1991).

(Men and women) who were part of the Azusa Street revival in 1906 in United States.[174]

This kind of Pentecostal-like revival Movements in India pushed aside the traditional western order of worship and hierarchy. In these revivals and experiences speaking in tongues was not seen as a primary evidence of the Baptism of the Holy Spirit or a requirement of missionary preaching as in classical Pentecostalism later on.[175]

Many early Pentecostals looked to Azusa as the fountainhead of the movement. Not surprisingly, when Alfred G. Garr and Lillian, newly Spirit- baptized missionaries from Azusa Street, stepped off the ship in Kolkata at the turn of 1907, they scarcely realized that Pentecostal or Pentecostal-like movements had already preceded them in India by nearly fifty years. Followed by them there were many missionaries including Robert F. Cook and his wife Anna Cook in 1913, Mrs. Mary Chapman in 1915, Spencer May in 1922 were also become the pioneers of Pentecostal revival in India. And there were many others who travelled across the country and preached the classical Pentecostal doctrine and became a witness for this great awakening.[176]

During this period large numbers of veteran missionaries embrace the Pentecostal faith. Among them a good number was women (Kate Knight of Christian and Missionary Alliance, Ramabai and Minnie Abrams of Mukti and many others) who made notable contributions in theological and missiological reflections.

The arrival of western missionaries and their wives paved a way for the establishment of many Pentecostal denominations such as Assemblies of God (AG), Church of God (full Gospel), Indian Pentecostal Church (IPC), and they started Bible Colleges. Currently these three are the leading Pentecostal denominations in India with their own theological and ministerial training centres. As a result of rapid spread of Pentecostalism, today there are many theological

174 Gary B. McGee, Latter Rain "Falling in the East: Early Twentieth-Century Pentecostalism in India and the Debate over Speaking in Tongues," 652.

175 Simon Samuel, "The Charismatic and Pentecostal Movements and their Commitments to the Social demands of the Gospel," 232.

176 Gary B. McgGee, Latter Rain "Falling in the East: Early Twentieth-Century Pentecostalism in India and the Debate over Speaking in Tongues," 649.

seminaries, missionary organizations and churches all over India. These emerging charismatic Pentecostal-like churches and socially and educationally empowering mission initiatives are in addition to the traditional Pentecostal churches. Such numerous named and innumerable unnamed charismatic and Pentecostal–like churches, socially and missionary empowering organizations now constitute the largest Christian constituency in India.[177]

The modern Pentecostalism has its following predominantly from the socially and economically refused and disposed segments of society. Most of its pioneers were from a racially segregated community. Many were named and unnamed women[178] who were committed to speaking in the church and engaging socially in empowering ministries.

The modern Pentecostalism began with a radical call to freedom from ecclesiastical oppressive structures, alienated episcopacy, unbiblical dogmas, traditions, beliefs and meaningless rituals, written down and antiquated liturgies and their emotionless, etc. In the place of a clergy controlled church life and worship, the Pentecostals introduced a wide variety of expressions of enthusiastic worship and prayer sessions where an ordinary believers who are filled with the Holy Spirit too took leading positions. In the Pentecostal churches, their spirituality is expressed through songs, spontaneous prayers and outbursts, prophecies, a narrative theology and testimonies. Though, some of the Pentecostal churches are slowly turning to become institutional and hierarchical,[179] in their popular and informal gatherings, the ordinary members including women who are filled with Holy Spirit and gifts of the Holy Spirit still take the lead.

Pentecostal and Charismatic movement in India made significant contribution in empowering and involving women in

---

177 Simon Samuel, "The Charismatic and Pentecostal Movements and their Commitments to the Social Demands of the Gospel," 232.

178 David G. Roebuck, "Cause He's My Chief Employer, Hearing Women's Voices in a Classical Pentecostal Denomination," in *Philip's Daughters, Women in Pentecostal-Charismatic Leadership*, ed. Estrelda Alexander and Amos Yong, (Oregon: Pickwick Publications, 2009), 38-60.

179 Simon Samuel, "The Charismatic and Pentecostal Movements and their Commitments to the Social Demands of the Gospel," 237.

Christian mission and ministry. The experience of baptism in the Holy Spirit and subsequent ministries such as preaching, prayer, etc., under the anointing of the Holy Spirit challenged to a great extent the gender differences in the church. This is not to suggest that the Pentecostal churches have many anointed women in higher realms of leadership and ordained ministries in the churches, but theologically and biblically a way is open for them to enter into leadership and play active roles in ministries. None can reject the fact that the Pentecostal movement grew and spread to the direct involvement of a good number of known and unknown and nameless women in ministry. Where ever the Pentecostal movement grew, there women along with men played very important leading roles. Some would even say that 'Pentecostalism globally has been framed by the ministry of Spirit-empowered women'.[180] Over half the Pentecostal congregations functioning by 1930 were established and led by women.

In other words, in the early Pentecostal movement, having the "anointing" was far more important than one's gender. As evangelistic bands carried the full gospel across the country, women who were recognized as having the anointing of the Holy Spirit shared with men in the preaching ministry. The early Pentecostal movement showed openness to women in ministry. The classical Pentecostal position holds that both men and women should be at all times fully open to the leading of the spirit. Believers share a responsibility to allow one another to function at all times "in the Spirit". The emphasis on "calling" and "gifting" in the Pentecostal movement superseded cultural and societal norms relating to the position of women and allowed them freedom in the exercise of leadership in the church.[181]

But as the movement transformed in to establish and formal structured churches, male dominated hierarchy developed within, and as a result women are neglected to the back seats to lead only auxiliary ministries and men occupied the prime places of leadership. The Pentecostal church now appears to be struggling between what Harvey Cox says a 'context between the fundamentalist and the

180 Simon Samuel, "The Charismatic and Pentecostal Movements and their Commitments to the Social Demands of the Gospel," 242.

181 A. Kay Fountain, "Where the Spirit of the Lord is," 34.

experientialist impulse,[182] that is' the experience of equality in the spirit is confronted by conservative Bible reading and theologies that insist on male leadership in the home and church.[183] Increasing institutionalization of the Pentecostal churches is leading to the suppression of the operation of the Spirit and of women to minister and lead. In other words of David Roebuck, 'with the church of God steeped in a tradition of separate spheres and a literal interpretation of Scriptures that seemingly prohibit women from serving as bishops and from usurping authority over men, their remains continued resistance to the idea of women serving as bishops or in governmental roles in the denomination.'[184]

Pamela Holmes laments: 'Pentecostalism, even with its denial of this world's ways and thinking, nevertheless has been enculturated to think within the modern world's value systems.[185] A recent observation shows that other than the Roman Catholic Church, the classical Pentecostal Churches appear to be emerging as the biggest male-dominated churches in the world.[186] The Spirit may be empowering women to preach, but the fundamentalist elements in the church are aborting the ministries of the prophetically called women. This to a large extent is setting the stage for stagnation, even decline, of many classical Pentecostal churches. Time has come for the classical Pentecostal to listen to and respond to what the Spirit is saying to the churches.[187]

---

182 Harvey Cox, "Fire from Heaven," 310.

183 Simon Samuel, "The Charismatic and Pentecostal Movements and their Commitments to the Social Demands of the Gospel," 243.

184 Pamela Holmes, 'The Spirit, Nature, and Canadian Pentecostal Women: A Conversation with Critical Theory' in *Philip's Daughters, Women in Pentecostal-Charismatic Leadership*, ed. Estrelda Alexander and Amos Yong, (Oregon: Pickwick Publications, 2009), 199.

185 Pamela Holmes, 'Spirit, Nature, and Canadian Pentecostal Women," 199.

186 Janet Everts Powers, 'Pentecostalism 101: Your Daughters Shall Prophesy' in *Philip's Daughters*, 135.

187 Simon Samuel, "The Charismatic and Pentecostal Movements and their Commitments to the Social Demands of the Gospel," 243.

### 2.2.2.2. The Place and Role of Women in the History of Modern Pentecostal Movement

As mentioned earlier, the beginning of the Pentecostal movement of the twentieth century is generally well recognized. The classical Pentecostal denominations owe their beginning to Charle's Parham's Bible School in Topeka, Kansas (1901), and that the first person recorded to have spoken in tongues in the twentieth century was a woman, Agnes Ozman, one of the Bible school students. This was the finest example of how God is using women in His providence for the extension of His Kingdom. There is also ample evidence that women took part in leadership in the beginning of the Pentecostal movement without any prejudice or objection. Many women played a large part in the early Pentecostal revival. Some of them gained wide reputation as preachers and writers. The basis for selection of leadership was divine calling rather than social or cultural propriety.[188]

From Azusa Street, Pentecostalism spread to other parts of the world by members who experienced the Pentecostal revival and formed Pentecostal churches. Azusa Street revival was a significant breakthrough in the theology that permitted the inclusion of women in ministry and leadership. Barbara Cavaness says women played vital roles of preaching and leadership at Azusa Street as well as receiving the blessing of the group as they carried the message across the continent and overseas. Of the first eleven elders of the Azusa Street Apostolic faith Mission six were women.[189] The early Pentecostals used the theology of Spirit baptism as the sole means of empowering for ministry. They believed that whoever received this empowering baptism of the Holy Spirit had an extraordinary call to minister irrespective of gender difference.[190]

The AG Church historian Gary McGee writes that the prominent role of women in ministry was characteristic of a revival where 'anyone could be chosen by the spirit for particular ministry.' Women became evangelists, pastors, and church planters. The

188 Deborah Gill cited by A. Kay Fountain; "Where the Spirit of the Lord is," 33.

189 Cavaneas, 'Leadership Attitude' in *Philip's Daughters*, 112-130.

190 Simon Samuel, "The Charismatic and Pentecostal Movements and their Commitments to the Social Demands of the Gospel," 242.

Pentecostal revival also opened doors in other cultures for women's leadership that was not possible at home. Soon after the outpouring of the Holy Spirit at Azusa Street, women were working as missionaries worldwide. After Pentecostalism the women missionaries became the founding missionaries of such Pentecostal denominations. The Pentecostal outpouring resulted in a much higher proportion of women in Pentecostal ministry than in any other form of Christianity at the time.[191]

Desmond Cartwright comments,

> My research seems to indicate that, women were an integral part in the 1901, birth of the Pentecostal movement, without them we might speculate that the Pentecostal revival might never have taken place..... Many of the most influential workers who were associated with Azusa Street were women: Among them are Lucy Pharoe, Mary Burges (founder of Glad tidings), Lucy Leatherman, Maria Woodworth Etter (founder of Wood Worth Etter Tabernacle at Indiana Polis), Emi Semple Macpherson (the famous woman preacher at USA, and the one who extend the financial help to R. F. Cook's missionary work in India), Florence Crawford, Clara Lum, Rachel Sizelove and four other single missionary women, Blanche Appleby who worked in China and Philipines, Lucy Leatherman, the first Pentecostal missionary to Egypt, Bernice Lee in North India, and Alice Wood in South America. They were free to travel and follow God's call like the early apostles without the demands of family. The workers from Azusa Street went out into all parts of the United States and sailed to the four corners of the globe.[192]

Desmond further states that women were the first to experience *glossolalia* in the west and those women were "particularly successful

---

191 Rosemarie Daher Kowalski, "The Mission Theology of Early Pentecost: Call, Challenge, and Opportunity," 267.

192 Desmond W. Cartwright, *Your Daughters Shall Prophesy: The Contribution of Women in Early Pentecostalism*, (Gaithersburg: MD, 1985), 2, 8.

in helping others into a Pentecostal experience. Thus, tongues became the accepted "preparation for missionary service and once baptized, all people, men and women, were expected to spread the gospel."[193]

There was an experience of infilling of the Holy Spirit in the Presbyterian Church at London, Reegatsswear in 1831 before 1901 experience (Perhaps we can say this as 'second Pentecost' and 1901 as 'Third Pentecost'). In that meeting, there was a woman named Mary Cambell who spoke in tongues. Pastor Edward Irving testify that after this incident Presbyterian Church turned to be like more than one of the Corinthian churches we see in the Bible. And he says, Mary Cambell was being send by God to bring revival in to my church.

Today, Pentecostal movement is being recognized by the world Christian bodies, including the world council of churches as a significant movement.

### 2.2.3. The Role of Women Leaders in the Mission of the Early Pentecostal and Charismatic Movement: Call, Challenge, and Opportunity

In this section, examples and case studies of missionary women from the first decades to the present will be presented. Future challenges facing women and their full participation in Pentecostal mission efforts will be identified. It will also explore the Pentecostal missionary women after the Pentecostal revival of the early twentieth century. It will include their responses to Pentecostal experiences and missionary carriers for about what it means to 'Go in to the entire world' as a Pentecostal.

The Pentecostal experience and reliance on the Holy Spirit was a significant part of Pentecostal women's call to and empowerment for missions, in facing the challenges of missionary service with Pentecostal eschatology.[194] Women, called by God, have played a large part in Pentecostal and Charismatic mission, but the question

193 Desmond W. Cartwright, *Your Daughters Shall Prophesy: The Contribution of Women in Early Pentecostalism*, 10.

194 Rosemarie Daher Kowalski, "The Missions Theology of Early Pentecost: Call, Challenge, and Opportunity," *Journal of Pentecostal Theology*, V. 19, 2 (2010).

of whether or not they will continue to do so represents a major challenge for the future.[195]

The history of women's role in Pentecostal and Charismatic movement is complex and contradictory. On the one hand, the Pentecostal tradition has often appeared far more open to women's preaching and leadership than have more mainstream Protestant churches such as the Presbyterians or Episcopalians. On the other hand, male Pentecostal leaders have just as often drastically narrowed the boundaries within which their female counterparts may speak and act in positions of authority, so that Pentecostalism has come to be perceived as far more conservative than mainline Protestantism on gender issues.[196]

The Pentecostal outpouring resulted more freedom besides interracial worship and service. It was a significant breakthrough in theology that permitted the inclusion of women in ministry and leadership. The Pentecostal women were allowed to exercise their spiritual gifts in the church and for the welfare of the humanity. These women formed their theology from their Pentecostal experience. They considered the baptism in the Holy Spirit a significant part of their call, permission to minister, and empowerment for missionary evangelism. Because of a Pentecostal eschatology of the imminent return of Christ, women were willing to endure a life time of discomfort, isolation from their own culture, and even death to reach the lost. They identified with the Biblical narrative, expecting the Holy Spirit to accompany their proclamation of the gospel 'with signs following' as in Mk 16:17-18 and in the book of Acts.[197]

Pentecostals have always believed strongly in the concept of the call of God. The Bible is replete with instances of Sovereign God calling men and women for His purposes. Often these persons of His choosing are the most unlikely candidates according to conventional wisdom. Paul Pierson goes as far as implying that most often revival

195 Barbara Cavaness, "God Calling: Women in assemblies of God Missions," 52.

196 W. E. Warner, "Women, Role of", *The New International Dictionary of Pentecostal and Charismatic Movements*, ed. Stanley M. Burgess (Zondervan: Library of Congress Cataloguing-in-Publication Data, 2002), 1203.

197 Rosemarie Daher Kowalski, "The Missions Theology of Early Pentecost: Call, Challenge, and Opportunity," 269-270.

and periods of missionary expansion have begun with people on the periphery of the ecclesiastical structures of their day. Often this leadership is provided by women. God chooses whom He will and extends His grace; it remains for the body to recognize that choosing. There were women who contributed their talents through writings brought great blessings to many.[198]

An early observer insists, 'Women did not push themselves to the forefront......God pulled them there. They did not take this ministry on themselves, God put it on them.' Jane Hunter says early women missionaries were 'daughters of the Second Great Awakening.... what most motivated women was their commitment to God and his calling, not personal ambition or adventure.'[199]

One of the major challenges women have faced in their ministry field is that although women played a vital role in the development of church and society, they have not been adequately recognized by the so-called 'male authorities within the church whether it be Catholic, Eastern churches, Protestants or Pentecostals. The patriarchal system or ideology and structures along with the male domination in the society have denied the women folk the opportunity to find out their own gifts and abilities and to appreciate their worth as a person created in the image of God. The attitude of the larger Indian society is also very much seen inside the church. It is not just the case with the Indian church alone. It has been the general attitude of the church universal. There have been various arguments in the history of the church to exclude women from leadership positions of the church. In spite of these hurdles, women have contributed to the welfare of the church both in this country and the church at large.[200]

It is quite right to say that the Pentecostal churches ensure the involvement of the women in the evangelising activities of the church, but they have failed to offer them the important positions in the church. They are given freedom to sing, to prophecy, to preach and to exercise their gifts in the church. They may be even appointed

---

198 Barbara Cavaness, "God Calling: Women in Assemblies of God Missions," 49.

199 Rosemarie Daher Kowalski, "The Missions Theology of Early Pentecost: Call, Challenge, and Opportunity," 268.

200 V. V. Thomas, "Contribution of Women to the Indian Church: A Perspective from the Pentecostal Churches in India," 169.

as the secretary of the women's fellowship. But it is to be noted that their voices are always controlled by the church leaders. The structure of Patriarchy plays a dominant role here. The male chauvinism is prevalent in the Pentecostal community. The women are considered as the inferior beings and are only subordinate to men in the family. The Pentecostal women do not enjoy equal status with men in the churches. The involvement of women is restricted to the areas of attending the worship service, exercising their gifts and involving in evangelistic activities. The traditional Pentecostals believe that the priestly ministry is set apart for men, and not for women. In the area of theological training the Pentecostal women have an emergence. The Pentecostals entertain theological training for women, but regret to say that they are not given many opportunities in the church to serve effectively. There is a prejudice against women in the Pentecostal churches in India.[201]

Almost up until the 1970s it was quite a normal thing to see the lower status of women in the Indian churches as it was part of the larger society where the patriarchal system dominated. As noted earlier the low status of women in the larger society definitely influenced the Indian churches to keep a subordinate place to women. Although, women formed the majority of membership in the church, they were not given place in the administration of the church or in the leadership positions. The ordained ministry was not given to them in almost all the churches except in few churches like the church of south India. But at the same time it must be noted although women were not given any position or the status as such, that did not keep women from contributing to the growth of the church.

Personal spiritual gifting and Charisma opened doors that had been closed to women for centuries, as Hunter observes, 'On occasion, especially talented women.....' have simply broken through the ideological binders of the tradition because of their extraordinary talent and their abilities to create large congregations and even social movements. Some women founded social programs or found creative ways to exercise leadership gifts in ways not offensive to male colleagues.[202]

---

201 M. Stephen, *Towards a Pentecostal Theology and Ethics*, 51.

202 Rosemarie Daher Kowalski, *The Mission, Theology of Early Pentecost*, 276.

However, in recent days compared to other traditions, the modern Pentecostal movement has been an exception to a large extent in its treatment towards women from its very inception. It is mainly because of the structure on which the Pentecostal movement is built. If women have contributed to the growth of the church, it is because of its free structure (although of late it is becoming more institutionalized), and the way they understand ministry.[203]

Therefore, it is certainly necessary for the church to affirm the concept of calling in order to utilize all the available labourers in the harvest. Pentecostals are the fastest growing Christian group worldwide, and very soon the vast majority of foreign missionaries will be Pentecostals. Unfortunately, the church in general has experienced a setback, due largely to the biased prejudices against women holding church offices. It is time for a movement to "take stock" if or when it starts exporting gender prejudices along with the gospel that threaten to stifle sovereign moves of God globally.[204]

### 2.2.4. The Role of Women and their Contribution in the Wider Pentecostal Movement

When we trace out the wider context of Pentecostal movement, especially in the west, however, the case was significantly different. From the very beginning of the Pentecostal Movement, women played an important role and their contribution has been well recognized. Women had crucial leadership roles in the development and spread of the movement. History witnesses to the fact that many pioneers of the Pentecostal movement were women. Today women have had extremely important leadership roles in the Pentecostal and Charismatic movements, as has been the case in most awakening and movements of spiritual vitality throughout Christian history.

The Pentecostal movement has been a significant part of twentieth century religion. Indeed, that movement ushered in the twentieth century, and the leading character was a woman. As I mentioned earlier the Pentecostal churches in the west promoted the women effectively to participate in the ministry. They offered wide

203 V. V. Thomas, "Contribution of Women to the Indian Church," 169.

204 Barbara Cavaness, "God Calling: Women in Assemblies of God Missions," 51.

opportunities for women, and some of the most influential voices in the early twentieth century were those of females. Their authority they believed came directly from God. Indeed it did not come from men, for the men in those churches were not necessarily any more eager to allow them positions of leadership than were men in the established churches. But at the very core of Pentecostal belief was the emphasis on the Spirit being poured out "on all flesh" (Acts 2:17).[205]

According to Edith Blumhofer, "In the early Pentecostal movement having the 'anointing' was far more important than one's gender. Their main focus was on the experience of the Holy Spirit baptism and the exercise of the gifts. Their experience of the Holy Spirit baptism gave them a new vision about ministry. Although, women had great freedom to preach at the beginning of the Pentecostal movement, the proportion of women in leadership dropped dramatically after 1920 until the time of the Charismatic renewal, when this trend was reversed. During this period (20th cen.) there were a number of factors favourable for the leadership of women among Pentecostals. But later the role of women in Christian ministry became more restricted due to several reasons.[206]

Another area in which Pentecostal women have contributed to the church has been through their prophetic ministry. There are number of women prophetesses in the Pentecostal churches. In the book of Acts we read about the sermon of Peter who quotes prophets Joel's prophecy concerning the demonstration of the Spirit in the latter days. In this the outpouring of the Spirit, the gift of prophecy is no longer to be the monopoly of a few in the past. It says your sons and daughters will prophecy. There is a radical-barrier breaking promise there. The pouring of the Spirit will result in the removal of all distinctions of age, gender, and social class. It is an egalitarian system which is brought forth here. The Pentecostal take this passage as the blue print for their ministry. Women's ministry in the Pentecostal churches also must be seen against this background of the account in the book of Acts.[207]

---

205 Ruth A. Tucker and Walter Liefeld, "Modern Pentecostalism and Denominationalism," 359.

206 Stanley M. Burgess, *Dictionary of Pentecostal and Charismatic Movements*, 898.

207 V. V. Thomas, "Contribution of Women in the Indian Church," 180.

Assemblies of God historian Gary McGee writes that the prominent role of women in ministry was characteristic of a revival where 'anyone could be chosen by the spirit for a particular ministry.' Women became evangelists, pastors, and church planters. Many of the missionary women have pioneered new fields, trained national workers, and spread the Pentecostal revival on every continent through evangelism and social ministries such as schools and medical missions.[208]

Women play key role in the development programmers of the church and other secular organizations. Some churches ordain women into the ministry of the church. Recently, Eggoni Pushpalalitha was consecrated as CSI Bishop of the Diocese of Nandyal. In our culture who can take the light of the gospel to the unreached millions of women? It is only the Christian women! But we cannot even talk of reaching other women until we understand their role and become aware of their responsibilities.[209]

Pentecostal women are often enthusiastic in sharing their Christian experiences on their own. Sometime this is done through counselling, praying, which eventually lead others to the church. Through such participation they are also an equal partaker in the building up of the body of Christ. Especially, during the time of crisis both in church and society, it is the woman who takes an initiative role to act as a prayer warriors in times of such situation. They were active in the evangelistic work particularly in the villages. There were Bible women or evangelists working on their own and that continues to be the case even today. These women were mostly unmarried with little or no training in the seminaries or *ashrams* and their basic contribution was to teach the basics of the Bible to the illiterate Christian women and to evangelize them. This has been one of the greatest contributions the women offered to the Churches although not recognized enough.[210]

208 Rosemarie Daher Kowalski, *The Mission Theology of Early Pentecost: Call, Challenge, and Opportunity*, 266.

209 Sakhi Athyal, "Transformation of Ministry Partnership Vision: Women and men Together as God's Agents of Transformation," *Journal of Theological Education and Mission*, Vol. 5, (2014): 42.

210 V. V. Thomas, "Contribution of Women to the Indian Church," 172.

If we think of a home without a woman, a neighbourhood, a church, a society, a nation or a world without women- we will realize the importance of women's presence and contribution. A woman totally yielded to God can be a powerful instrument in God's hand for transformation. The church need to realize the strategic role women play in bringing cites to the Lord. The great commission of Jesus Christ in Matt: 28:16-20 is for every Christian to obey and fulfil. So women cannot be excluded. Sometimes, new converts especially women are eager to share their new found faith in Christ with other women.[211]

In a country where men have always been at the forefront, and have always been the leader, discussion on the women in mission or as change agents in the history of the church might appear a little out of place to some. However, historical evidences provide ample examples of women who have impacted change in the history of the churches at enlarge and continue to initiate and influence change at all levels in the church.

Let me pen down the names of great servants of God who contributed a lot and their greatest ministerial impact in the wider mission field, mostly looking at women who have made a difference, and women who have led the way. My attempt is to stick to the examples found in the history of the church.

Woman recognized the personal spiritual gifting and Charisma that lead them to opened doors that had been closed to women for centuries. On occasions especially talented women have simply broken through the ideological binders of the tradition because of their extraordinary talent and their abilities to create large congregations and even social movements. Some women founded social programs or found creative ways to exercise leadership gifts in ways not offensive to male colleagues.[212]

The Mission history must replete the heroic examples of the women. There were many who dedicated their lives (both western and Indian) for the growth of Indian church and served the Lord in the educational field as teachers, in Medical missions fields as doctors like Hilda Lazarus, Ida Scudder, Mary Varghese and in social

211 Sakhi Athyal, "Women and Men together as God's Agents of Transformation," 43.

212 Rosemarie, *The Mission, Theology of Early Pentecost*, 276.

services like Amy Carmichael, Mary Roy, Aruanà Gnanadasan, etc., and there were women who were involved in the arena of theological education with theirs different capacities. Along with the western missionary women, Indian women too played an important part in the nurture and growth of the church in India. Amy Carmichael is even today considered to be one of the greatest missionaries. Ida Scudder is still remembered as one of the pioneers in the medical mission in India.[213]

One of the Indian Christian women who played a significant role in God's mission is Pandita Ramabai of Maharashtra. She stands at the top of the list of women who made a strong impact in Church history. She is considered as a "Builder" and "Mother" of Modern India. Her mission contributions are manifold. She is also a pioneer in the emancipation of women. She was an ordinary woman with intelligence and creativity. Ramabai's choice represented an audacious challenge to men. When she committed her life to Christ, she was used by God abundantly. She is an example to the great contribution that women rendered to the Indian mission.

One of the most famous women leaders that have emerged in the last century in our country is Mother Teresa. She is known and addressed as 'The Saint of the Gutters'. She did what she felt 'called by God' to do. She became a pioneer as a modern day saint for compassion and service to the poorest of the poor.[214]

Many western missionaries were models of ministry for Indian women. A good number of them were involved in the ministry of the church, but very little is known about most of them. Some of the western missionaries wrote about a few of the Indian women who helped them with their ministries, but these reports are very few.[215] There are both single and married women have served as church planters, evangelists, doctors, nurses teachers and pastors in the far-flung corners of the world. They were gifted and anointed for specific tasks, and that was more important than credentials and human authorization.

213 Sakhi M Athyal, *Indian Women in Mission,* (Bihar: New tech Printers, 1995), 83.

214 Geeta Mondal, "Women as Change agents in Indian Society," *Dharama Deepika*, June (2005): 65.

215 Stan Guthrie, "A Woman's Place in Missions," (Global report), 6.

Ruth Tucker observes that,

> It was that nebulous and indefinable "missionary call" that impelled them to move out. If ministries in the homeland could be pursued without a "call", foreign missions could not. The stakes were too high. And it was that sense of calling, more than anything else that was the staying power.[216]

It is against this backdrop that we could look at the lives of few women pioneers who joined the ferment of the times and through their action and involvement left an indelible mark on the life of a church in the throes of great change and revival.

So far we looked at women from worldwide who were representative of the significant contribution to the early Pentecostalism and additionally, several outstanding women were among the many evangelists and missionaries who went out from western countries to take the message of Pentecostalism across the country and around the world. In much of the historiography of Pentecostalism, these women's name and legacies have been all but forgotten. This was the case even to the Indian women who worked tirelessly behind the growth of the church in India as general and Pentecostal church in particular. As I have mentioned earlier, since male leaders have dominated the historical record, the roles of these women have been basically ignored and they have largely remained unnamed.[217]

### 2.2.5. Some Important Women in the Pentecostal Churches and their Contributions

At this juncture, it is important to have a study on the lives of charismatic and Pentecostal women ministers/ leaders who played a key role to promote this Pentecostal faith. There are several

---

216 Ruth A. Tucker, *From Jerusalem to Irian Jaya* (Grand Rapids, MI: Zondervan Publishing House, 1983), 487.

217 Estrelda Alexander, "Introduction," in *Philip's Daughters, Women in Pentecostal-Charismatic Leadership*, ed. Estrelda Alexander and Amos Yong, (Oregon: Pickwick Publications, 2009), 5.

missionary women from England and America who came to the Indian continent. The modern missionary movement has a record of numerous women who made great achievements in different spheres of Christian mission in the world. With this respect, it is worth mentioning that there were also some women evangelists in Kerala, always been at the forefront witnessing of Jesus Christ and will continue providing their incalculable contributions in the third millennium, just as they did in the first two. Women have always been the backbone of the missionary effort. They were the women of faith.

While we will mention some of the prominent ones, we should not forget, there are many stories of the unsung and uncelebrated women, whose battles are just as great, just as painful, and just as rewarding. We may hear of them, or we may not, but they are there and they will continue. Let us look at the lives of some of the women who through the last few centuries brought about a change in the early Pentecostal movement.

History witnesses to the fact that in the west, many pioneers of Pentecostal movement were women, including Florence L. Crawford, Marie Burges Brown and Aimee Semple McPherson, etc. Some, such as Maria B. Woodworth-Etter and Carrie Judd Montgomery, had already established ministries during the nineteenth-century Holiness Movement. There had been a strong tradition of women in leadership in the Holiness movement. Phoebe Palmer had been pivotal in its development and Hannah Whitall Smith was another woman leader.[218]

If Charles Parham/William Seymour are recognized as the founder of the modern Pentecostal Movement, it was a woman, within the context of the twentieth-century Pentecostal movement, who first received the baptism of the Holy Spirit with the gift of tongues. She was Agnes N. Ozman, and with this, the modern Pentecostal movement was born. Another incident of speaking in tongues was witnessed by one of the girls at Mukthi Mission run by Panditha Ramabai. This news was reported as one of the most celebrated

218 Stanley M. Burgess, in *Dictionary of Pentecostal and Charismatic Movements*, ed. Stanley M. Burgess and Gary B. McGee, (Michigan: Zondervan Publishing House, 1988), 893.

events of the great revival in India. Some of the most important early accounts of these events were written by women, such as Parham's wife, Sarah Parham and her sister, Lillian Thistlethwaite. From 1901 onwards there were many women functioned as important leaders. Another important woman, Mrs. Mary A. Arthur, began her service through healing ministry.[219]

Minnie F. Abrams served as a missionary in India from 1887-1912. She is known as the leader in the 1905-1906 spiritual awakening. She trained and promoted women evangelists. She also wrote the popular work 'The Baptism of the Holy Ghost & Fire' to promote the need for a post-conversionary experience of purification and empowerment for effective evangelism. She was the most prominent of the veteran missionaries who moved from the women's missionary movement through the ranks of the holiness movement to Pentecostalism. Though few evangelicals and Pentecostals would recognize her name today, Christians in India and America hailed Minnie Abrams as a leader in revival and evangelism. Unfortunately, the contributions of Holiness and Pentecostal women to mission have frequently been overlooked or underestimated. In the case of Abrams, historians have mentioned her name only briefly in connection with the revival in India and her contribution to the Pentecostal Methodist movement in Chile.[220]

There were two missionary ladies in Kerala who worked along with the first Pentecostal missionary who came to Kerala in 1909. They were Miss Bouncil and Miss Aldi Wingil. They came originally as Brethren missionaries but after the experience of infilling of the Holy Spirit they turned as Pentecostals at Coonoor. There were other women who contributed immensely such as Sister Bernice Burges, Miss Martha Kusera, and Miss Eddy. And another person to be noted is the wife of R. F. Cook named Bertha N. Cook. She has contributed greatly to the women among the early Pentecostal Churches in Kerala.

In the very beginning of the Pentecostal movement in Kerala there were women who took big steps for the sake of gospel and

219 Stanley M. Burgess, *Dictionary of Pentecostal and Charismatic Movements*, 897.

220 Gary B. McGee, "Baptism of the Holy Ghost & Fire!: The Mission Legacy of Minnie F. Abrams," *Missiology: Tools of the Trade*, Vol. xxvii, 1, (1999): 515.

most probably would have paid the price for it. But they did it. Their sacrificial love and strong commitment made them to do so. Many single missionary women had been treated in a different way. They were not permitted to do anything that others did. In the midst of all such challenges women persuaded their spiritual journey and used the gifts God had given them and served as role models for Pentecostal movement. Several women have helped in the evangelistic ministries as helpers and partners to their husbands.

As mentioned, there are number of Pentecostal women from within India especially in Kerala who have involved in the ministry of the church and contributed greatly to the church. But very little is known about most of them. Some of the missionaries wrote about a few of the Indian women who helped them with their ministries. Others wrote about those they admired, but even these reports are very few. There were several missionary women, women evangelists effectively to participate in the ministry. They are usually called Sanyasinis (Women ascetics). But they were not ordained. Most of them were active in the evangelistic work particularly in the villages. They were Bible women or Evangelists working on their own and that continues to be the case even today. These women were mostly unmarried with little or no training in the seminaries or Ashrams and their basic contribution was to teach the basics of the Bible to the illiterate Christian women and to evangelise them. They are the late Annamma Mammen, Pennamma Sanyasini, soshamma sanyasini, Saramma Thomas, Prophetess Kalayapuram Annamma, Aleyamma Kunjummen, Mrs. K. E. Abraham (Annamma Abraham) affectionately known as Sara Ammachi or Hebron Ammachi, Mrs. Annamma Chacko, Mrs. Mariamma Samuel, Mrs. Mariamma Thomas, Mrs. Rushiamma John, Aleyamma Mathew, Mrs. Mary Kovoor and Vazhoor Thankamma.

Thankamma is being remembered by her home town as Vazhoor Thankamma. Her name is highlighted as I know her very personally. She was a prophetess who ministered both in Kerala and in different parts of India. She is 'The forgotten story of a Female Prophet.' Her name is not included in the writings of many Pentecostal male historians in Kerala. She was a very important person in the lives of many men and women of God, who is serving the Lord faithfully and successfully even today in the northern part of India. She has been an inspiration to both men and women of God. Many male historians are selective in what they can place in a work and they made sure few of them were included in the pages of Pentecostal history and others are not. If we had only male prophets we would never even know many female servants of God existed. But I want my readers and the ministers of God to recognize her greatness (along with other men and women of God). Thankamma is a best example who influenced many women of God serving the Lord in ministry today. She is being an approved prophetess of the Lord. She was consulted by number of great men and women of God in the history of Pentecostals. They are mainly George C. Kuruvilla, T. S. Sam, K. J. Kuriakose, and P. V. Joseph. As per her guidance and direction they received clear confirmation from the Lord to persuade their spiritual journey regarding their initial period of ministry from south to the northern parts of India. Today all of them are immensely used by God and became a great men in the northern parts and abroad and they all are serving the Lord in his vineyard in a best possible way.[221]

### *2.2.5.1. Annamma Abraham*

In 1921, while Annamma Abraham was working as an elementary school teacher, Pastor K. E. Abraham, founder of Indian Pentecostal Church of God, married her. Later she resigned her job and spent full-time helping her husband in his ministry. She empowered many women. She was a strong prayer warrior and supported pastor K. E. Abraham and his co-workers in fasting and prayer in order to fulfil the great vision God had given to them. Her dedicated life, life model, prayerful life, hospitality, the burden for the perishing soul, concerns for the church were the factors which made the ministry of Pastor K. E. Abraham as great blessings to tens of thousands in India and abroad. As most of the time Pastor K. E. Abraham was on missionary journeys, Annamma very efficiently looked after the Bible school and the matters related to Church. She walked scores of miles with other sisters, evangelists and pastors and made an entry into homes which would have otherwise shut to the gospel. She

221 From Clara M. Shiju, a close associate of Vazhoor Thankamma.

organized camps for the ladies and also started a ladies bible school during mid-summer vacation days in order to encourage and equip women for ministry. She was always working behind the scenes, not expecting any publicity or fame.[222] She was a pious and exemplary mother and also a mother to all the members of the church. She cared for the Indian Pentecostal church like her own family. The Indian Pentecostal Church in India and abroad can never forget her valuable service.[223]

### *2.2.5.2. Annamma Chacko*

Annamma after her studies at Nicholson High School in Thiruvalla, became a life partner for Pastor P. T. Chacko in every sense of the world. She trained up her four daughters and only son to live for the Lord. Besides her household duties, she often visited the homes of the sick and prayed for them. She preached to the women in English and Telugu. She opened her home for visitors from every background. She was a prayer warrior and was never idle for the Lord. She exercised the gift of healing through healing ministry. She brought a group of untouchables to Christ. She was promoted to glory in 1964.[224]

### *2.2.5.3. Aleyamma Kunjummen*

Aleyamma became the wife of Kunjummon Daniel. Since 1950 Mrs. Aleyamma has given untiring service in the training of young women for the Lord's ministry, as matron of women from 1950. She played an important role in shaping their lives for the ministry. Though she was born in the Syrian Jacobite church, God in his mercy filled her with the Holy Spirit and fulfilled her desire to become a true witness. She recalls the faithfulness of God over the years and delivering her even from the point of death.[225]

---

222 T. Valson Abraham, "Mrs. Annamma Abraham Empowered many Women," *Revive*, Vol. 11, 2015, 4.

223 T. Valson Abraham, "Trumpet: Faith of our Fathers," 1.

224 T. Valson Abraham, "Trumpet: Faith of our Fathers," 1.

225 Finny George,"Karthavil Niryatayaya Mrs. C. Kunjummen," *Assemblies of God Doodhan 41/12* (August, 1995): 16.

### *2.2.5.4. Mariamma Samuel*

Mariamma was the wife of P. M. Samuel. She had four sons and two daughters. While her husband travelled, she prayed and by giving prayer and moral support she helped him in his ministry. Sickness and troubles did not discourage her from following the Lord. She knew how to console the poor and suffering folk. Young men and women gained practical training in ministry and life when they stayed with this family.[226]

### *2.2.5.5. Aleyamma Oommen*

Aleyamma is married to K. C. Oommen, an evangelist. After her conversion, she began to witness to her family. Her husband teased her, but from then on she was a different person. She becomes witness by visiting homes and preaching in meetings. Her main method of preaching was sharing her own testimony and telling how God had changed her as a person. She was also a good singer and composer of gospel music. She had a team of singers who communicated the message of the gospel through music. She first worked in an orphanage. Since, she was a woman she has to face lot of oppositions in her ministry. But she was a courageous woman. Through her ministry several men and women got converted and her example led many women in to ministry. Kunjamma Joseph is an example of one who joined Aleyamma in her ministry. Pattam Mariamma, Ponnamma Sanyasini and Joy Sanyasini came to know the Lord through her ministry and became full time evangelists. Her ministry lasted until 1967. She had the gift of prophecy. God used her in Kerala, Tamil Nadu and Sri Lanka. When God calls women, and they have the courage to oppose the injustice of the society, God help them to fulfil their ministry in the church.[227]

### *2.2.5.6. Annamma Mammen*

Annamma after her high school education went for teacher's training. After her training, while she was working as a teacher, through vision she experienced God's definite call as a fulltime minister. After that

226 T. Valson Abraham, "Trumpet: Faith of our Fathers," 22.

227 Sakhi M. Athyal, *Indian Women in Mission*, 46, 48.

she had an experience of infilling of the Holy Spirit in her life. She had travelled to many countries with the Gospel. Except Australia, she had travelled almost all countries and preached the word of God. Not only that at times she (is an emigrant) holds the citizenship of country like Israel and Honk Kong. She pursuit knowledge in English, Telugu, Tamil, Kannada, Hindi, Hebrew, etc. and later served as the vice Principal of "Truth Bible Institute." Through her exemplary life and ministry several women and men committed their life for missionary service and several of them been strengthen in their faith. In the beginning of Pentecostal movement in Kerala her contribution towards the women's ministry is unforgotten. Annamma Mammen and Mary Amma (wife of Ashtamudi ummanchen) gave leadership for founding *'Sankethem'* (house for staying unmarried women). Mangalasery Mariamma, Keeprayar Annamma, Kalliseriyil N. K. Pennamma were the first women's group who stayed in these Sankethem and they were actively involved in propagating Pentecostal faith to others. Later Annamma Mammen became a renounced woman preacher, missionary woman and has obtained the knowledge of composing several Malayalam revival songs like "Lokamam Gambeera Varidhiyil," and "Uyarthidum Njan ente Kankal." These songs have inspired and touched many lives and still remained as songs of inspiration in our hearts and minds. Though, she passed from this world at the age of 90, but the songs impacted change and continue to penetrate our hearts and minds. The famous Bible scholar, Rev. Costa Deir says, Annamma Mammen was her spiritual Mother.[228]

### *2.2.5.7. Aleyamma Sanyasini*

Aleyamma was a woman of prayer. She fasted and prayed much. Those were her greatest weapons for her ministry. She remained single all her life, and lived a very simple life style. She was well accepted by the people.[229]

228 Saju, *Kerala Pentecosthu Charithram*, 228.

229 Sakhi, Athyal, *Indian Woman in Mission*, 72.

### *2.2.5.8. Pennamma Sanyasini*

Pennamma Sanyasini dedicated her whole life as a woman ascetic for God's service. She was a woman with a difference. She was born as a Marthomite believer in the year 1908, January 20th. Later in 1922, by hearing the message of Sadhu Kochukunju Upadeshi she surrendered her life for full time ministry. She joined his band and wore saffron cloth. Though, Upadeshi was against women preachers, but he accepted Pennamma Sanyasini and encouraged her in ministry by giving her supporting hands. Later in 1934 she left Ashram and started Indian Gospel team. Meanwhile, she was filled with the Holy Spirit and became a Pentecostal believer. She travelled from place to place along with her team and proclaimed the gospel. This method of ministry was very effective. Through her ministry many men and women became full time evangelists. Throughout her life she led a very simple life, and travelled all over the world. She stood as a living witness for her saviour. Though she was a Malayalee but very rarely visited Kerala. Most of her ministry was out of Kerala like Tamilnadu, Bangalore, and Andhra Pradesh, etc.[230]

### *2.2.5.9. Mary Kovoor*

In her initial period of ministry Mary Kovoor worked along with Bethel Ashram. Later she joined the Bible College in Bangalore for her theological training. After her training, in the year 1958 she took water baptism and the following year married to a pastor named Kuruvilla from a famous Kovoor Marthomite family. In 1963, her husband too obeyed the commandment of God took water baptism, and later both of them took decision to serve as a full time ministers. As a result they established an Independent Pentecostal church in Kavumbhagam closer to their house. Later numbers of churches (around 11) were established in south India. Like many other pioneers, this couple toiled tirelessly, keeping prayer and word of God as their focus in their life. Their life and ministry impacted thousands of people. After so many years of faithful ministry for the

---

230 T. G. Johnson, "Munpe nadannavar, Munpil nayichavar", *Halleluah, Pentecostal Year Book*, ed. Samkutty Chacko Nilambur, (Thiruvalla: Plensy Sam Publisher, 2015), 212.

Lord, due to their old age and ill health, Mary Kovoor is taking rest at her residence in Thiruvalla, Kerala.

What is even more encouraging is that their children are ministers of the gospel. Their son George Kovoor, who is a Neuron Surgeon by profession, is an amazing preacher of the word of God. God is using him in an incredible way for the expansion of His Kingdom. Her daughter Sarah Kovoor resigned from her job and is fully engaged in ministry along with her husband A. K. George, a Cardiologist residing in Missouri in States. Both of them are pastoring a congregation at Missouri. God is using Sarah as a mighty preacher in different places.[231]

### *2.2.5.10. Lillykutty (Annamma) Samuel*

Lilly Kutty Samuel is another excellent single woman preacher's in today's Church. She is invited to many conferences and meetings in India. She was born and brought up in a Syrian Jacobite family in Kerala. She came to the Pentecostal experience through her brother Simon Samuel (Principal of NTC, Dehradun). God is using her very powerfully in the city of Bangalore and other parts of Kerala. Under her leadership they organized a 'women link' to have a social network in connection with all other women in Kerala and other parts of India. Through this link they are trying to reach out to the unreached to the other parts of India. She had a team of sisterhoods in which women serves as evangelists and full time workers. Recently she is ordained as a full time minister from the IPC church, Bangalore.[232]

### *2.2.5.11. Anna Kandathil*

Anna Kandathil is the daughter of a former Thiruvalla Muncipal Council's Chairman K. M. Mammen Mappilla and Grand Daughter of Kocheapen Mappilla of Malayala Manorama (Kerala News Paper). She came to the Lord in 1998. She is powerfully used among

231 Interview with Sarah Kovoor (Daughter of Mary Kovoor pastoring at AG church in Missouri, USA) at New Life Bible College, Cheruvakkal, Kerala on 17th June 2015 and T. G. Johnson, "Munpe nadannavar, Munpil nayichavar", 264.

232 Information collected from Simon Samuel, principal of NTC, Dehradun, on 30 July 2015, at NTC, Dehradun.

Malayalis community throughout the Globe. Some of her powerful public sermons are 'Impact of Christ birth upon the Family', 'Do not harden your hearts', 'God's Chosen Servant', 'Lost Inheritance', 'New Covenant', 'True Victory', ' Can these bones live', and 'Jesus will Judge', etc.

There were several other women who were active in the evangelistic work and contributing to the growth of the church. There were Bible women or evangelists working independently and that continues to be the case even today. These women were mostly unmarried with little or no training in the seminaries or ashrams and their basic contribution was to teach the basics of the Bible to the illiterate Christian women and to evangelise them. This has been one of the greatest contributions the women offered to the churches although not recognized enough. Saramma Thomas was an amazing woman who took in charge of one of the Ashrams known as 'Bethel Ashram in Trichur.' After her death it was run by Aleyamma Jacob.[233]

---

233 Saju Mathew, *Kerala Penthekosthu Charithram*, 228.

Chapter 3

# The Status and Roles of Women in the Present Day Assemblies of God in General and Kannur District in Particular

## Introduction

We shall look at the beginning of AG church work in Kerala and then at the different stages of history in the growth of AG church in Kerala. This will help us to know the efforts of the western/ national missionaries who were part of this movement. They had to sacrifice a great deal-comforts, conveniences, financial security, and several other things. The story of many of the Travancore women missionaries was also not different. Therefore, it is necessary to study and understand what made them a recognizable force in establishing and shaping the AG churches in the region during its early phase.

## 3.1. A Brief History of the Assemblies of God in Kerala

The history of the AG church[234] abounds with examples of missionaries both (men and women) who paid the ultimate

234 In my first chapter the researcher had given a glimpse of the brief history of AG church, that may not be sufficient and appropriate to understand the role played by many individuals especially women and men both (western and

price for their faith and laid down their lives for their saviour. This is true in the story of the AG church in Kerala too, where missionaries ventured into this land, knowing that their very lives are at stake. Many of them met with untimely death, some in the most unusual manner. But the gospel lived and by the first half of the 20th century, the missionaries, many of them were women, left their mark on the mission field making an extraordinary impact. A number of women missionaries became a part of the rapid growth and enthralling development of the AG church in Kerala. Their lives, work, and influence spilled over, in particular, into the early part of the twentieth century.

The first one to bring the clear teaching of Pentecost to south India was George Berg, an American missionary. Berg worked in different parts of Kerala beginning in 1901. He was not a Pentecostal missionary at that time and had dissension in the discussion of his conviction of speaking in tongues.[235] In 1908, Berg returned to the United States and was baptised in the Spirit at the Azusa Street Mission and spoke in tongues. Again he was invited to preach in the Brethren convention at Kottarakkara in 1909.[236] Berg came to Kerala again in 1912 with Robert F. Cook, a young missionary and the first Pentecostal church was pioneered at Thuvayoor, Adoor.[237]

During this period Cook had a group of charismatic and committed young native preachers (men and women) as his co-workers. Daniel Ayroor states that at this occasion the arrival of Chapman as a great support and inspiration to Cook in his ministry.[238] More over all those who worked with Pastor Cook during this time became outstanding leaders of different Pentecost groups later. Their

---

natives) missionaries, who came as pioneers in the first quarter of the twentieth century.

235 A. C. George, "Pentecostal Beginnings in Travancore, South India," 234.

236 Saju, *Kerala Penthacosthu Charithram*, 30-31.

237 Rosewell Flower, *Origin and Development of the Assemblies of God* (Springfield: Gospel Publishing House, 1952), 6.

238 Daniel Ayroor, *Keralathile Pentecosthu Sabhakal* [Pentecostal churches in Kerala], (Mavelikara: Beersheba Bible College, 1985), 45.

joint efforts resulted in the establishment of scores of churches in Travancore.[239]

Pastor Cook started his Pentecostal venture in India in 1913, as independent missionary. He writes this:

> We landed in India without a set program, nor had we any promise of support, save $ 5.00 which my father, promised to send each month, providing the Lord prospered him. In this way I served the Lord in India for 7 years, before I was led to join up with the general Council of the Assemblies of God...... I am sure that it was God's will for me to affiliate with them....[240]

It may be noted from his words, that he had joined the AG church after seven years of independent service in India, i.e., in 1920.

In 1922, Cook moved to Kottarakkara with his family and continued the work. The following years Cook and his wife Bertha laboured tirelessly in Travancore for 37 years from 1913-1950 establishing many churches in different parts of Travancore.[241] Bertha was a woman of many talents. She has contributed greatly to the women among the early Pentecostal Churches in Kerala. When Cook started the Mount Zion Bible School in 1928 at Mulakuzha, it was Bertha who headed the school as Principal. Cooks oldest daughter Blossom also served as missionary in India.[242] Cook's affiliation with the AG church and subsequent settlement at Kottarakara with his family made commendable advancement in the AG work in Kerala.

All these changes contributed notable progress in the history of AG church in Kerala as a denomination, in the beginning of the third decade of this century. Since then, Pentecostalism spread out its wings both in central and south Travancore under the influence

239 Mathew P. Skariah, *An Evaluation of the Assemblies of God Church in Kerala and Proposals for the Unity among the Pentecostal Churches in Kerala*, (Unpublished thesis), FFRRC, Kottayam, 1996), 61, 91, 94.

240 Robert F. Cook, *Half a Century of Divine Leading and 37 years of Apostolic Achievements in South India*, (Tennesse: Church of God, 1955), 126.

241 A. C. George, *Trail Blazers for God*, 199.

242 A. C. George, *Trail Blazers for God*, 199.

of AG denomination. From that time onwards AG church made promising development in Kerala.[243]

There was a setback for AG church in the Central Travancore when Pastor Cook and his family detached their association with the AG in 1929. They left the movement with several churches and all the properties so far acquired in 1926 by the help of the AG general council.[244] The Cooks were officially related and supported by the AG Foreign missions Department, until they were separated from the same in 1929.[245] This was a severe blow up on the AG work in Kerala. However, timely supply of missionaries from the division of foreign missions and emerging national leadership conceded the work to continue. The years after the great set-back marked remarkable progress in the history of the AG church in Kerala. More missionary force also was added in to the mission.[246] In the following years capable and anointed men and women took up and provided able leadership to the church all over south India. Pastors like A. C. Samuel, C. Manasseh, C. Kunjummen, P. D. Johnson, and P. S. Philip extended their valuable service for the movement and at present under the able leadership of Rev. T. J. Samuel, AG moves on to register an unprecedented growth.[247]

## 3.2. The Status and Role of Women in the Formation of Assemblies of God in Kerala

This section will investigate exclusively on the status and role of women in the formation of AG church in Kerala. History witnesses to the fact that from the very beginning of the Pentecostal Movement women were central to the discourses and practices created and sustained among enslaved and churches. Their roles in the growth and development of Pentecostalism (AG) have not been fully described

243 L. Sam, "Assemblies of God Annum Munpathiel" (Assemblies of God is always in the fore front), *Assemblies of God Messenger*, Vol. 41, no. 6, (1955): 14.

244 Mathew P. Skariah, *An Evaluation of the Assemblies of God Church in Kerala and Proposals for the Unity among the Pentecostal Churches in Kerala*, 74-77.

245 n.a., "Report," *Pentecostal Evangel*, (July 21, 1926), 3.

246 Carl F. Graves, "Encouraging News from South India," *Pentecostal Evangel*, (February, 1933): 9.

247 K. J. Mathew, "A Century of Potential Witness," 12.

and appreciated. Therefore, this section focuses on the integral role of women in the shaping of the AG church in Kerala. They played an important role and many pioneers of the Pentecostal movement were women. Even in the midst of Patriarchal opposition, women carved out roles that actually fostered the growth of churches and the advancement of a movement. They exercised a spiritual agency that contradicted the use of Biblical admonitions for women to be silent and invisible. At the same time they utilized the Bible to defend their participation in church leadership.

Throughout most, if not all, of the history of Pentecostal missions married and single women missionaries have constituted a majority. According to Thomas E. Trask the General Superintendent of the Assemblies of God in America, women have contributed greatly from the very beginning to the Pentecostal movement. He says "if you were to look at our history, women have made some of the most outstanding contributions to the AG church in foreign missions, home missions, pastoral positions, evangelism, and as teachers. The fellowship would not be where it is today if it were not for the ministry women have given to this church. In fact, the first General Council of the Assemblies of God in 1914, recognized the role of women in ministry generously than most evangelical denomination at that time."[248]

This is true in Kerala too. There were a good number of women who have contributed greatly to the church and graciously gave themselves in reaching out many lives for the Kingdom of God. They all responded to the call of God on their lives by demonstrating that they were dependent on the Holy Spirit in spite of gender limitation. However, most history books do not share the great achievements and contributions of the amazing women who have established many churches, shaped families and brought transformation in many lives. All these attempts through the Spirit of God which is poured on all flesh would accomplish this. The echoes of their testimony can still be proved that God never intended for woman to stay behind veiled curtains, locked away from the responsibility. Instead throughout the history they proved the equal responsibility given to them and that they are able and capable, dependable and trustworthy in their

248 Thomas E. Trask, "Ask the Superintendent," *Enrichment,* Spring, (1997), 8.

responsibility that God equally wants to use them as instruments of peace and messengers and as leaders. Those women played a predominant role and made a great impact towards the establishment and growth of the AG church in Kerala.

The following section will explore the ways women in the AG church contributed to the growth of the church. The arrival of Mildred C. Ginn and Lydia H. Graner had been a great encouragement to the missionaries and the national workers in the south parts of Travancore. They were authorized ministers of the AG church, who extended their faithful missionary service by establishing Bethel Bible School.[249] Their extensive sacrificial commitment to uplift the young ladies in society and make them known the love of Christ proved through the participation and enrolment of women in the Bible School. Almost one fourth of the enrolment in the Bible school was women. As a result many Indian ladies were trained and used in the ministry. After their training period they served the church in different capacities such as evangelists, Sunday school teachers, Pastoral assistants and so on.[250] By the first half of the 20th century, number of women missionaries came from west, such as Mary Chapman, Constance Swinfen Eddy, Mary Lindburg, Martha Kucera, Lydia H. Graner and Mildred C. Guinn, etc. During this period the participation of women in the ministry of AG church also was highly appreciable.[251]

From time to time more missionaries were added in to the ministry of the Bible school. In December 1927 Bernice F. Andrews joined the mission after her marriage with Burgess. In 1930, Miss. Mildred C. Ginn arrived at Quilon where she worked in an orphanage until 1934. Then she moved into Bethel Bible School at Mavelikkara. Later missionaries like Mrs. And Mr. Clarence Maloney joined the missionary force in 1935. In 1937 another missionary lady, Lydia Graner from USA joined along with Ginn and ministered in the

---

249 A. C. George, *Trail Blazers for God*, 210.

250 Earl and Arlene Stubbs, *The Assemblies of God in South India*, (Unpublished paper), 1974, 13.

251 Archives Collections from Punalur Assemblies of God Museum.

school until their retirement in February 1972.[252] The Bible school teachers and the students actively participated in the practical mission work, along with their assignments in the school.[253] New stations were started in different parts of central Travancore by the efforts of the Bible school. As per the reports, by the end of 1934 there were fifteen Assemblies and fourteen pastors in the central Travancore.[254]

It is not possible to give a profile of all those who were used by God in the growth of the AG work in Travancore. Nevertheless, few name both native and westerner women missionaries need to be mentioned will be highlighted. The name of Mrs. Aleyamma Kunjummen, Miss. Kunjamma, Miss. Saramma and others are praise worthy.[255]

### 3.2.1. Constance Swinften Eddy

C. S. Eddy was born on 28 January 1875 in England. She was ordained by E. N. Bell in 10th August 1914. She came to India in 1928 and worked in different parts of South India.[256] She worked in Trivandrum, Konniyoor and Mavelikkara. When South India and Ceylon District was formed in 1929, she was elected to the post of secretary treasurer. She was re-elected to the same post in the general conferences of 1933 and 1935.[257] The earliest Pentecostal works in the northern parts of the Malabar was started by Eddy in the year 1930.[258] In 1932, the main mission station was opened at Kannur,

252 John H. Burgess, "Bible School Proves Blessing," *Pentecostal Evangel*, (May 18, 1935), 6.

253 John H. Burgess, "Bible School Proves Blessing," 6.

254 Mathew P. Skariah, "An Evaluation of the History of the Assemblies of God Church," 81.

255 V. Sunitha Jasmine, *Women's Role in Building and Nurturing the Assemblies of God Church in Kerala* (Delhi: ISPCK, 2013), 65-66.

256 Archieves Collections from Punalur Assemblies of God Museum.

257 V. Sunitha Jasmine, *Women's Role in Building and Nurturing the Assemblies of God Church in Kerala*, 49.

258 Santhosh John, "Malabar District Vibhajanaum Anubentha khadagangalum (Division of Malabar District and its immediate reason)", *Aathmaniravinte Nooru Varsham:* A History of Assemblies of God in Kerala, Editted by Finny George, Published by AGMDC, 2015, 82-87.

known also as Hebron Mission.[259] Mean while AG work progressed in the Malabar area. In 1934, Eddy was able to establish a church in Kannur. It was here that Eddy had the opportunity to display her gifts. She taught classes for children and adults, engaged in open-air preaching and took the important step of starting door-to-door visitation, and reaching those whom the church neglected.[260] Above all she directed her energies towards stirring up the hearts of young men and women to volunteer for the mission field in Kannur. She recognised that the native peoples would be able to take over their own church growth. She was stirred and motivated others into action and mission of God quickly established in this belt. Another area of Eddy's mission involvement was her keen interest to work among the prisoners in the town. There she tended the wounded and persuaded the prisoners to return back and won many converts especially women.[261] She visited the prison along with her co-workers, shared the love of God, conducted Sunday schools; counselled the prisoners, and enquired about their living conditions, health and happiness. She became a regular visitor to the prison and was able to share the gospel with them. It is reported that many men and women responded with enthusiasm. As a result there followed a number of remarkable conversions, such a way by the help of the nationals her work progressed immensely._She always promoted the natives, both men and women in the ministry. [262]

### 3.2.2. Winnie P. Nilland

On 13th October 1927, Winnie was assigned as a missionary to South India. On November, 1927 she landed in India. In the following year she paid her first visit to the South India and attended Ceylon District Council Conference. As a result of this link she was chosen as the secretary-treasurer, in the third conference held on 3-4 July, 1931.

259 N. A. "New work blessed in South India", *Pentecostal Evangel*, (August 12, 1933): 11.

260 Archives Collections from Punalur Assemblies of God Museum.

261 C. S. Eddy, "Blessings in South India", *Pentecostal Evangel*, (September 22, 1934): 4.

262 A. C. George, *Trail Blazers for God*, 59.

She persuaded her work while staying at Quilon and surrounding areas.[263] She pioneered work in Nellikunnam and Thevalakkara.[264]

### 3.2.3. Martha M. Kucera

Martha Kucera was born to a missionary family in Czechoslovakia in the year 1900. Her parents dedicated her to God even before she was born. From her childhood, she had a love for God and her interest in missionary work developed at an early age. After Martha's initial days of education her family moved to United States and there she completed her higher education.[265] Realising the call for ministry, she joined for theological training in a Bible school. She experienced the missionary call and been inspired by a God- given compulsion to 'preach the gospel of Jesus Christ'. Probably as a response of God's call she came to India in the year 1928.[266]

Martha's first tour of ministry proved quite successful and lasted for 33 years in India. She settled in Trivandrum, travelling around the country and ministering to different people groups especially Hindus in Kerala. Meanwhile, she familiarised herself with area and visited other mission stations of women in their homes.[267] Kucera loved to work along with the natives, as she felt more at home with the natives, she found the natives accepted her, and as she shared their difficulties, sought her help and advice. She felt that this form of evangelism was more effective than preaching. She spent most of her time in caring the poor and needy for their physical needs around the surrounding areas.[268] The natives marvelled at this display of the love of God in her.

263 Archives Collections from Punalur Assemblies of God Museum.

264 T. J. Samuel, "Keralathil Pravarthicha Videsha Missionarimar: A.G. Missionarimar", *Halleluah: Pentecostal Yearbook,* ed. Samkutty Chacko Nilambur, (Thiruvalla: Plensy Sam Publisher, 2015), 278.

265 K. S. Samuelkutty (ed.) "The Missionary Lady Who Preached in Malayalam in the Capital City," *Assemblies of God Doothan* 49/ 1 (September 2002): 11.

266 K. S. Samuelkutty (ed.) "The Missionary Lady Who Preached in Malayalam in the Capital City," 11.

267 Martha M. Kucera, "Report," *The Pentecostal Evangel*, (August 19, 1933): 4.

268 Archives Collections from Punalur Assemblies of God Museum.

Martha learned Malayalam language and surprised others at the speed with which she picked it up and her fluency in preaching Malayalam was remarkable. She eventually became so fluent that she knew not only the colloquial phrases and the inflections, but gestures as well.[269] Moreover, she was also able to assist the preaching. Such was her love for the people. There were many converts and most of them were from Hindu background. In 1933, she had reported about a baptismal service in which there were twelve participants.[270]

Martha quickly became involved in outreach programme and closely worked with the national brethren. She loved and encouraged them in the ministry. It was through her effort Pastor A. C. Samuel joined in AG church. God used both of them very effectively to establish many churches in the Trivandrum area.[271] She received ordination from the east district of America on 23 April 1936.[272] Her physical condition did not allow her to travel freely and to involve actively in the ministry. Once she fell and broke her spine. This incident left her invalid for the rest of her life. Rest of her life she was more or less confined to her room, yet from her chair she continued her role as teaching the pastors, listening to their problems. She kept in touch with the outside world through her next few years of ministry in India.[273] Throughout her struggles in India, Martha was always aware of her strong dedication and commitment to the Lord.

Due to her sacrificial love and initiative for the people of India, in memory of Martha, the AG church parsonage erected at

---

269 Martha M. Kucera, "Report," 13.

270 Martha M. Kucera, "Report," 13.

271 K. S. Samuelkutty (ed.) "The Missionary lady who preached in Malayalam in the Capital City," 11.

272 V. Sunitha Jasmine, *Women's Role in Building and Nurturing the Assemblies of God Church in Kerala*, 45.

273 V. Sunitha Jasmine, *Women's Role in Building and Nurturing the Assemblies of God Church in Kerala*, 45, Sheeba James, *The Ministry of Women in Pauline Writings and its Relevance in the Present Day Churches in Kerala with Special Reference to the Assemblies of God, Bethel Bible College*, (An unpublished Thesis), 91.

Cheruvakkal.[274] This is only a small reminder of the missionary lady who loved the nationals and enjoyed preaching to them in their own language. Even though, she wanted to continue her ministry in India, on 1961, the Foreign Mission Department asked her to return back to the United States. Seven years later on 13th of November 1968 she passed into God's presence very quietly.[275]

### 3.2.4. Mary Lindburg, Hellen Lenert, Essler and Alta B. Hodge

Mary Lindburg, another missionary lady came to India in 1928 and remained in India until her death. She worked from 1937 in South Travancore to strengthen the AG work.[276] On 3rd September 1936 another woman missionary named Helen Lenart, came to South India. She stayed and worked with Mary Lindburg for quite some times. Later she went back to states.[277] During World War II, when many missionaries returned home, she chose to stay back in the field, no matter what may come on her way.[278] After her departure in 1948, Miss Ellen E. Essler came to Thiruvanthapuram as a young missionary. She was overseeing the AG church work in Thiruvanthapuram. She was appointed as a Sunday Schools supervisor in the churches.[279] In 1953, there were two other missionaries, Miss. Alta B. Hodge and Essler joined with her and there ministry was real blessing to the churches. Pastor M. Johnson of Vizhavoor, the first president of the South West District C. A. Movement helped them in interpreting their messages.[280] Miss. Essler and Miss. Hodge moved to Trichur-Palakkadu stations in the year 1954. After few years, Miss. Essler

274 A. C. George, *Trail Blazers for God*, 207.

275 "The Missionary lady who preached in Malayalam in the Capital city" *Assemblies of God Doothan* (September, 2002), 11.

276 L. Sam, *A.G. Charithra Rekhakal*, Assemblies of God Malayalam District Council, from 1913 to 1927, 21.

277 Archives Collections from Punalur Assemblies of God Museum.

278 K. S. Samuelkutty (ed.) "Assemblies of God in South Travancore", *Assemblies of God Doothan* 48/9 (May, 2002): 17.

279 L. Sam, "Miss Hodge & Miss Essler- Two Missionary Ladies", *Assemblies of God Doothan* 48/10 (June, 2002): 19.

280 L. Sam, "Miss Hodge & Miss Essler- Two Missionary Ladies," 19.

returned home and spend her later years of retirement in the United States. Miss. Hodge continued her teaching ministry in the SABC Bangalore, where she was acknowledge as an able and respected teacher. After a long career in the college, she went back home and spend her retirement in the States.[281]

### 3.2.5. Miss. Mildred C. Ginn and Miss. Lydia H. Graner

Miss. Mildred Ginn and Miss. Lydia Graner knit together in friendship while they were studying in Southern California Bible College.[282] They recognized the need to train women missionaries, particularly in India. Especially in Kerala, the traditional barrier was prevailed during those days, where native women were generally kept out of sight in a male-dominated world. Such circumstances lead them to found the urgency of a female approach was acceptable to break the barriers.

Mildred Ginn came first to India in 1930 and joined with Burgess at Mavelilikkara. Looking around for ways of being useful to God, she undertook a great responsibility to became a dedicated woman to train young people especially women for the Lord. To attain this goal, she associated with Bethel Bible School, Punalur to be fully involved in training young women.[283] During her stay in Kerala, she learned Malayalam. Typically, it was Mildred Ginn saw the need to train young ladies who were more easily able to approach to Indian women and break down the barriers.[284]

Another missionary lady was Lydia Graner. She was born on 1906 into a middle class family in Seattle, USA. Her parents were God-fearing Baptists. Her father was a Pastor. She was deeply moved and decided to spend her life in 'loving God with all her heart.'[285]

281 A. C. George, *Trail Blazers for God*, 221.

282 L. Sam, "Assemblies of God Malayalam Districtum Videsha Missionarimarum (Assemblies of God Malayalam District and Western missionaries)", *Aathmaniravinte Nooru Varsham: A History of Assemblies of God in Kerala*, ed. Finny George, (AGMDC, 2015), 99-108.

283 Mildred Ginn and Lydia H. Graner, "God's Noble Vine" *Golden Jubilee Souvenir,* (1927): 7.

284 Lydia H. Graner, *Assemblies of God Doothan*, (November, 2001), 14.

285 Lydia H. Graner, *Assemblies of God Doothan*, 14.

Her interest for missionary work developed at an early age when she heard a sermon by a woman preacher named Mrs. Macpherson. The sermon created a deep impact on her life. At that moment God filled her with His mighty power and she surrendered herself fully to the Holy Spirit. She heard God's call and committed herself to His will. Whenever she prayed, the word 'India' came to her life.[286] She seized up the opportunity to come to India as a missionary and started to pray in earnest about the trip. A few days later God answered her prayer, gave her the money for the trip. In 1937 she reached India and immediately joined with her friend, Mildred in ministry.[287] By the arrival of Lydia Graner from USA, in 1937, the teaching faculty of Bethel Bible College was strengthened. Lydia and Mildred joined together along with other faculty, had developed a strong sense of responsibility in the Bible school. However, the arrival of both missionaries marked the beginning of a new way of partnership with the Bible College. They were drawn together in a determination to serve Christ. Mildred and Lydia were ordained ministers from AG church.[288] They both together ministered at Bethel.

In the next few years the Bible School teachers and the students actively participated in the practical mission work, along with their assignment in the school. These foreign missionaries were closely associated with the national leaders and supported them all throughout the years. As the work expanded, Bethel Bible School became the centre of all the activities of the AG church. Mildred and Lydia remained in the Bible school at Punalur till their retirement in 1972.[289] The women missionaries who worked in Kerala in this period were more associated with the church growth activities unlike other parts of India. Missionaries in the Bible School were less institutionalized.[290] They were involved in systematic evangelistic

---

286 Mildred Ginn and Lydia H. Graner, "Students on Evangelistic Tour", *World Challenge*, (October, 1957): 7.

287 Lydia H. Graner, *Assemblies of God Doothan*, (2000): 15.

288 Mildred Ginn and Lydia H. Graner, "God's Noble Vine," 7.

289 Mildred Ginn, "Report," *Pentecostal Evangel*, (September 27, 1947): 8 and Interview with Dr. Issac V. Mathew, Christian Counselor.

290 John H. Burges, "Bible School Proves Blessings" 6, Lydia H. Graner and Mildred C. Ginn, "Another forward step" *Pentecostal Evangel*, (March 4, 1951): 12.

activities and pioneering churches. As the work expanded, Bethel Bible School became the centre of all the activities of the AG church. During this time the 'Home Missionary Council' emerged as the evangelism department of the Bethel Bible School, commenced in the early fifties of this century, for missionary outreach. Most of the AG churches in Kerala were established by the effort of the HMC. M. S. Mathai observes that the seventy five percent of the AG churches in north Kerala as the result of the HMC endeavour. [291]

They taught an entire generation of ministers in the Assemblies of God Malayalam District. The students trained during those years had become pillars of the church in Kerala and other states in India and abroad. These women missionaries were held in high esteem for their deep knowledge of the word of God and their excellent communication skills by their students.[292] These great women of God were given a warm farewell by the South West District Council of the AG on its conference held at Trivandrum on January 27, 1972. After the completion of 42 years of ministry in India, on 17th November 1980 Graner went to be with the Lord and Ginn passed away after completing 38 years of ministry in India.[293]

### 3.2.6. Miss. Bouncil and Miss. Aldivinkle

In 1980, two missionaries Bouncil and Aldivinkle came to South India and received the baptism of the Holy Spirit. God used these missionary ladies in a remarkable way to spread the Pentecostal message to various parts of South Travancore.[294] During the year, it happened, they had a vision regarding Mrs. Manasseh and Pastor Mannesh who were facing problem because of their faith. God led these women missionaries to Paraniyam, the residence of this missionary couple. They extended them all the support and help they

---

291 Martha Kucera, "Bible School proves Blessing", *Pentecostal Evangel*, (May 18, 1935): 13.

292 Mathew P. Skariah, *An Evaluation of the Assemblies of God Church in Kerala and Proposals for the Unity among the Pentecostal Church in Kerala*, 69, 91, 94.

293 Sheeba James, *The Ministry of Women in Pauline Writings and its Relevance in the Present Day Churches in Kerala with special reference to the Assemblies of God*, 92-93.

294 Saju, *Kerala Pentecosthu Charithram*, 57.

needed.[295] God used them as an instrument in leading this couple to Pentecostal faith. Later, they became the first native Pentecostal preacher of South Travancore.[296]

Apart from these missionaries, the churches had lot of occasional visitors from different parts of the world. Later many missionary families like, Bernice and Burges (1927) Robert Shaver and family (1950), Ernest A. Sorbo and Mrs. Philis Sorbo (1951), C. Earl and Arlena Stubbs (1975) and many others joined and contributed very much to the AG work in Kerala.[297] The vision, dedication and service of these missionaries were still greatly admired. The service of the national ministers to the school is also highly appreciable. There were missionaries who were sent by other denominations and joined the Assemblies of God Church later.

## 3.3. The Role and Ministry of Native Women Missionaries in Assemblies of God in Kerala

The AG church in Kerala had many native women who were involved in the growth and development of the church in Kerala, though they were not in the limelight. Even though, these women played an important role in the history of AG church in Kerala, we cannot see much historical records regarding their contributions. Foreign women missionaries were models of ministry (for both native men and) women, but it is surprising to find out that the native women missionary were treated differently.[298] Foreign women missionaries had freedom and were given due respect both in Bible College and Church activities, which was not so for the Indian women. They were not permitted to do many things unlike foreign women missionaries.[299]

Therefore, it is important to know how they used the gifts God had given them, and how they served as role models for the

295 L. Sam, "Keralakarayile AG Missionarymarekurichu Oru Anusmaranam", *Assemblies of God Malayalam District CA Golden Jubilee Souvenir* (2001): 23.

296 A. C. George, *Trail Blazers for God*, 251.

297 C. Kunjummen, "The Early History," *Bethel Bible School Golden Jubilee Souvenir*, (1977): 4-5.

298 Sakhi M. Athyal, *Indian Women in Mission*, 18.

299 Sakhi M. Athyal, *Indian Women in Mission*, 18.

entire society. A good number of native women missionaries played an important part in the growth and development of the churches in Kerala. They too deserve to be added in the history of AG church in Kerala.

I would like to point out some of the native women of God in Kerala who were involved in various types of ministries. They travelled around the villages and visited the houses of women who were not exposed to the outside world. They were women who have been mightily used by God in different ministries.[300] They were ordinary women- housewives, mothers, teachers and daughters. When God called them, they submitted their lives to Him, and God used them powerfully. The western missionary women trained these native women and took them on evangelistic tours.

In most of the places in Kerala, women were the first fruits who very soon became the messengers of the gospel. They shared this good news in their own family and became witness to their people. Later some of them got married to pastors and evangelists and consistently bear witnesses by planting more churches.[301] Some of them sacrificed their personal desires for the sake of gospel and continued in ministry remaining single.[302] Their sacrifices and toils for the growth of the Assemblies of God work in Kerala had been unveiled and we do not see much record of their contribution in the history of AG Church.

### 3.3.1. Sheelal Manasse

Sheelal was born and brought up in a LMS family, in Chennai as the daughter of Perinba Muthu. She was married to Evangelist Manasseh. Manasseh was a self supported Evangelist and preacher in LMS at that time.[303] The Spirit filled ministry of Ms. Aldwinkle and Ms.

---

300 Helen Kooiman Hosier, *100 Christian Women who Changed the 20$^{th}$ Century*, 303.

301 Sakhi Athyal "Women and Men Together as God's Agents of Transformation," 46.

302 Leelamma Athyal, *Man and Woman: Towards a Theology of Partnership* (Thiruvalla: Christava Sathya Samathi, 2005), 80.

303 L. Sam, "Pr C. Manasseh Thekkan Thiruvtamkurile Adyathe Penthakosthu Susrushakan," Pr. C. Manasseh the first Pentecost Minister of South Travancore, *Assemblies of God Doothan* 40/1 (September, 1983): 5.

Bouncil led these couple to the Pentecostal faith.[304] Later they got baptised in water and received the Spirit Baptism. The LMS church excommunicated them and removed them from their community. Their ministry in their own native place and other areas yielded fruits for God's kingdom.[305] They were regarded as pioneers of AG work in the South Travancore. Both were committed in learning the word of God.

Sheelal was a school teacher in Marthandam Government Girl's High School. As a midwife she rendered free service to many local women irrespective of their caste or religion she used to visit all the houses. In spite of her busy schedule in the school, Sheelal, proved her God given talent and potentiality as a renounced woman preacher during those time.[306] She was very much involved in the ministries like house visiting, conducting prayer cells, etc. More than a woman missionary, Sheelal was a woman who made friendship with the public and won their respect and love. She worked tirelessly in many places. That often paved the way for pioneering evangelist work in some areas. Her well-respected life made Manasseh to become more successful in his ministry.[307] Through her prayer one of her colleague, named Thankamony teacher got healed miraculously. This incident brought the entire family into Pentecostal faith, and it resulted the beginning of AG church at Plantope, Puthukkada.[308] She engaged most of her time and energy among the ladies and cared so much to win them for Christ. Manasseh and Sheelal worked very closely with Mary Chapman. Their strong commitment, dedicated life served as an inspiration and support for many to stand firm in their faith. These couple left a good legacy for the believers to cherish. In the

---

304 A. C. George, *Trail Blazers for God*, 252.

305 A. C. George, *Trail Blazers for God*, 252.

306 L. Sam, *A.G. Charithra Rekhakal*, SIAG Malayalam District Council Souvenir, 23.

307 A. C. George, *Trail Blazers for God*, 252.

308 L. Sam, "Pastor. C. Manasseh the first Pentecost minister of South Travancore," *Assemblies of God Doodhan*, 5.

year 1970, she went to be with the Lord.[309] Today, many churches are established in this area.

### 3.3.2. Aleyamma Kunjummen

Aleyamma was born as a single sister of five brothers to Mrs. & Mr. Koshy Panicker and Aleyamma Panicker. She was brought up in a Syrian Jacobite family in Kundra. She came to the Pentecostal faith through her brother. Her heart desire to serve the lord in ministry was fulfilled when she married to pastor Kunjummen. She earned her theological training, and did ministry in various ways. Aleyamma played a crucial role and was a backbone to her husband's successful and powerful ministry.[310]

Aleyamma served as a matron of the Bethel Bible School for girls. She gave much attention to girls and treated them as her own children and gave special care for them. She undertook a number of activities in order to uplift them. She played an important role in shaping their lives for the ministry. Her opening move was to start a tailoring school for the ladies so that they could be taught to knit and sew. The women responded her move with enthusiasm. In this way the women learned a little self-respect.[311]

Aleyamma continued to look for other ways of making herself useful to God and was responsible for uplifting number of ladies in the society. With the help of a group of ladies she visited hospitals and provided clothing for the sick women and children and also prayed for them. Through this ministry, she brought many of them to Christ. She was inspired by her faith in God and her conviction that all human beings whether they are rich or poor should be treated with equal and respect. On 20th July 1995 she died peacefully.[312]

---

309 Annamma Johnson, "AG and Women Workers," *SIAG, Souvenir: A Publication of the Malayalam District Council,* (2000), 83.

310 Finny George, "Karthavil Niriyatheyaya Mrs. Aleyamma Kunjummen," *Assemblies of God Doothan* 41/12 (August, 1995): 16.

311 Aleyamma Kunjummen, "Report," Assemblies of God Bethel Bible College Golden Jubilee Souvenir 1927-1977, 13.

312 Aleyamma Kunjummen, "Report", 85.

### 3.3.3. Kunjamma- Saramma Sisters

These two sisters hailed from an ordinary family, in Charummood near Kayamkulam. At a very early age they separated their life for the service of God. They both remained single and invested their maximum time and energy for the expansion of God's kingdom. Their main ministry was conducting tarrying meetings in different places. Through these meetings many received the baptism of the Holy Spirit and were instrumental in bringing back many back sliders into strong faith.[313] It is said that they spoke with marvellous effect, and that the pathos of their voice melted even the hardest hearts. As a result hundreds responded to the gospel. They travelled to every nook and corner of Kerala to propagate the Gospel. Their simple way of life impressed the Pentecostal believers, and they become a role model to them.[314] Since these both sisters were associated with AG church in Kerala, AG church honoured them by giving credential. AG history of Kerala, always remember the significant role of these missionary sisters who sacrificed their life for the growth and development of AG church in Kerala.[315]

### 3.3.4. Susannamma Papachen

Another outstanding woman was Susannamma sister. She was born to a Christian parent from Kerala. Her father was Pulimoottil Philippose and her mother Rahelamma. She was married to Mr. Papachen in 1948. She got converted through the ministry of her husband. She took water baptism on 31 July 1961 and became a member of the AG church, Anchal.[316] She started ministry by visiting homes and conducting prayer meetings. Through her preaching many people both men and women received Jesus. Her exemplary

313 N. A. "Kunjamma- Saramma Sahodarimar" (Kunjamma- Saramma Sisters), *Assemblies of God Women's Missionary Council Souvenir* (1983), 42-43.

314 P. N. Zacharia, Assemblies of God Sabhakal: Arambhavum Valarchayum Ente Ormayil, *SIAG, Souvenir*, (2000), 45.

315 Annamma Johnson, "AG and Women Workers," 84.

316 Raichel Daniel, "Nammude Missionarimar," *Assemblies of God Doodhan*, 52/2 (October, 2005), 37.

life led many women into ministry.[317] She had the gift of healing, prophecy, casting out demons and many other gifts. God used her in Kerala and many other surrounding areas. She was very prominent in the gift of prophecy during those days.[318] She exercised all these gifts and ministered along with her husband in different parts of Kerala. God used her in an extraordinary way to plant churches in Aroor near Anjal and nearby areas. Since they belonged to AG, both of them were given credential as authorised ministers by AG. More over AG church gave ample opportunities to this couple to minister in different churches. In the year 1980 she went to be with the Lord.[319]

### 3.3.5. Kodangavilla Sisters

Kodangavilla sisters are Kamalam, Jagathamma, Baby and Thankam. They worked together in Thiruvantapuram region. They were very effective in ministry.[320] Sister Kamalam came to faith through miraculous healing, then others followed the footsteps of Kamalam and joined with her in ministry, and they became famous women ministers in that area. As they were faithful to God's call, He helped them to fulfil their ministry that God had entrusted upon them.[321]

On one occasion Kodangavilla sisters held a prayer meeting in which many sick were healed, and many demons were cast out during that meeting. God did an amazing work through these sisters and brought a great revival in that place. As a result, in 1972 God enable them to start Sunday worship with the help of some of the believers of Kollam AG church. Today this church is known as the Kodangavilla AG church.[322] God honoured them by calling and

317 Annamma Johnson, "AG and Women Workers," 24.

318 Annamma Johnson, "AG and Women Workers," 24.

319 Raichel Daniel, " Nammude Missionarimar," 2000, 39.

320 Annamma Johnson, 'AG and Women Workers,' 23.

321 Interview with Pastor Finny George at Bethel Bible College, Punalur on 5 January, 2015, and Archives Collections from Punalur Assemblies of God Museum.

322 Interview with Mrs. Mariyamma Samuel, wife of Pastor T. J. Samuel, (Superintendent, AG Church), President of the Women Missionary Council, at SIAC, office, Punalur, on 5 January, 2015.

using for pioneering many AG churches in Thiruvananthapuram. They ministered in AG churches in Kerala, Bangalore, Mumbai and Chennai.[323] Through their ministry many became full time evangelists. God used them as prophets and preachers. In the initial time, they were assigned as full time ministers conducting even marriages and funeral services.[324] They have been invited as main preachers in many conventions. Neither they were highly educated nor they had any Bible school training yet by their simple faith and self-sacrificing zeal, God enabled them to be effective and powerful ministers for the Lord. Kodangavilla sisters remained faithful until their death.[325]

### 3.3.6. Couple Ministers

There are many native couples who helped together in the evangelistic ministries as helpers and partners to their husbands and worked tirelessly for the Kingdom of God. Among them, few are enlisted below:

#### *3.3.6.1. Kunjamma Paniker*

Kunjamma Paniker was the wife of pastor Paniker, one of the most gifted early leaders of the Assemblies of God in Kerala. Within this short span of time, God used them in a tremendous way and contributed much to the AG church.[326] Mrs. Kunjamma's support and encouragement made him to become a successful minister for God. She was a woman of prayer warrior, a strong inspiration and wise woman of God always willing to stand beside her husband with counsel and prayer. Because of Kunjamma's commitment to prayer, her husband was strengthened and was mightily used by God in ministry. "Prayer, she believe, is her greatest resource to bring about

323 V. Sunitha Jasmine, *Women's Role in Building and Nurturing the Assemblies of God Church in Kerala*, 62.

324 Raichel Daniel, "Nammude Missionarimar, Malayalam Districtle WMC Pravarthanangal," 38.

325 Annamma Johnson, "AG and Women Workers," 23.

326 L. Sam, "AG Charithra Rekhakal," 12.

change."[327] Leaving his wife and children behind, Paniker died in 1949 at the age of 35 and went in the presence of his Lord whom he had loved and served so faithfully. Though his ministry lasted only for a few years, but God had given a similar vision to his wife, Kunjamma. As a result she carried out of the responsibility of leading the work faithfully.

Kunjamma had her assignment from God, though the authorities of Bethel Bible College forced her to stay back in Punalore. In 1950, she and her children moved to Chamavilla house, their native place in Kundra and settled there.[328] Since they did not have any spiritual gathering in that area, it was her desire and dream to pioneer a church in Kundra. She started to pray over this matter. Soon God's leading became clearer. With the help of AG authorities and Pastor P. N. Sakharia who has been appointed as an in-charge of that work, in the following year, they could start a Pentecostal church in that town. Today this AG church is known as the first AG church in Kundra.[329] Even after the departure of her husband God has fulfilled all the promises He has given to Paniker through his wife and children. Until her death she remained as a missionary and worked tirelessly for the Lord.

### *3.3.6.2. Marykutty Thomas*

Marykutty is from Karunagapally. She got married to Pastor K. M. Thomas. They both worked very sincerely and actively for the sake of Pentecostal faith. They were full time ministers of God in the AG church. She too became an immense prayer support for his husband's ministry.[330] They used to visit believers homes and shared the love of Christ to them and bring many of them to Christ. Her hard work and dedication to her God earned the love and respect from her people and became a role model for them. She found out the

---

327 Assemblies of God Prarambhanethruthrayam, An interview with Dr. Y. Jayaraj (about early prominent Pastors: Rev. A. C. Samuel, Pastor K. M. Paniker, Rev. C. Kunjummen) by Mulavana Mohan Das, 160.

328 Assemblies of God Prarambhanethruthrayam, "Mrs. Kunjummen- Kunjamma Paniker, 33-34.

329 L. Sam, "AG Charithra Rekhakal," 27.

330 Annamma Johnson, "AG and Women Workers," 23.

freedom and acceptance of the warm hearted people, who permitted her to be "just a part of the church."[331] As a prophet God sent her abroad and many other places in India and she is been known as one of the prominent woman preachers in those days.[332] Her ministry was helpful for the growth of the AG church in Karunagapally and surrounding areas.

### *3.3.6.3. Aleyamma John*

Another couple was Aleyamma, wife of Pastor Iype John. They worked in Kerala and served God very faithfully for a number of years. Mrs. Aleyamma took an important role in home and raised their children in a God fearing manner. As a result all of them are serving the lord as fulltime ministers.[333] They both shared the same vision and served with total commitment. In this way she worked along with her husband and fulfilled the call of God entrusted upon them.

The above mentioned families are only representative of the early workers of the AG church in Kerala. Through this they proved that women too can play a key role in propagating the Gospel provided they have a burden and passion for the perishing souls. In this prevailing culture, she is expected to be under the care, protection and leadership of her husband.[334] Intercession is a form of ministry that the Lord has bestowed to ladies, which is the greatest of all ministries.

According to Mrs. Aleyamma Thampy, wife of Pastor V. A. Thampy (founder president, New India church of God), the president of the women's ministry of the church, who is serving for past 43 years in Christian ministry made a beautiful statement in connection with the role of women in ministry, 'When you see a building, nobody sees the basement, but only the building. That

---

331 Missionaries worked in Kerala, South Indian Women serve (Archives collection from Punalur AG).

332 Finny George, "AG Yile Chila Adhyakala Pravarthakar", *SIAG, Souvenir*, 2000, 57, L. Sam, "Keralakarayile AG Missionarymarekurichu Oru Anusmaranam," 23.

333 Annamma Johnson, "AG and Women Workers," 81.

334 Mariamma Thampy, "Women and Prophecy: Role of Women in this Ministry," *Revive* 7/2 (January-February, 2014): 12.

is what ladies (wives) are doing- they lay the foundation for the building.[335]

In fact in no way we should undermine the potential of a woman in mission. All should understand the reality that God can use anyone provided they are committed servants of God and truly sensitive to the call of the Holy Spirit. "Ministry" as I understand it, if a husband and wife realized the call and commitment and the passion that they left everything for the sake of God's Kingdom they both can shared the same vision, dedication about being in the ministry. There are many unknown women in AG church, who contributed immensely and did outstanding work for the expansion of God's Kingdom, but unfortunately they are hardly brought to limelight by the male historians, but the eternity historian records the scenes behind the curtains. I strongly argue and underline the fact that when both husband and wife are actively involved in mission, ministry will become exceedingly effective.

### 3.4. Women's Missionary Council (WMC) in Kerala

From the beginning of the AG church in Kerala, women were active participants in the growth and development of AG work in Kerala. Even in the local churches their contribution is very well remembered. The ministry of the missionaries encouraged them as well. In local churches, the wives of the pastors or some able women lead women's meetings. More over this ministry was concentrated within the local churches. So there was a need for an organisation for women at the state level. For this purpose, and with the initiative of great women, (Kunjamma Daniel, Mariamma George, Annamma Johnson, Shallini Pallickal, Mariyamma Samuel, Mary Sam, Raichel Daniel, Leelamma Daniel) through Assemblies of God church the women missionary council started in Kerala. Today they have these units in all the AG churches in Kerala. In most of the churches, the wives of the pastors served as leaders of WMC.

This wing is also known as the ladies department of the AG church, constituted by its motto 'We serve as unto the Lord'. During the early ages of Assemblies of God, most of the women

335 Annamma Thampy, "Women and Prophecy," 13.

missionaries joined together and actively took part with one accord to make a successful venture.[336] They actively partook in spiritual as well as humanitarian aspects of the church. On 22 December 1975 a conference was conducted for women at Plamood Assemblies of God Evangelistic Centre. This conference was mainly for the wives of the pastors in the Trivandrum region. As a result many of them joined together and made a vow to work hard for the Lord. For the smooth functioning of this ministry, they formed a committee.[337] It was first given by the name 'Sodari Samajam' (Society of Sisters). Mrs. Annamma Johnson was elected as president, Mrs. Mary Sam as secretary and Mrs. Vimala Robinson was the treasurer. During this meeting a decision was made to gather together once in two months. Later in 1976, February 28, another conference was held at Thirumala AG church. In that meeting this Sodari Samajam renamed as Women's Missionary Council (WMC). Within a year WMC spread to other churches of Kerala and all other sections in the district came under Women's missionary council. An annual conference is also held at Punalur for women and special meetings for women were held at the section and regional levels as well.[338]

In 1982 December 15, the Assemblies of God executive committee announced Mrs. Annamma Johnson as the women's missionary council president. From that time onwards anniversaries, camps and other meetings were conducted district wise. In 1992, Mrs. Mariamma Samuel became the president of WMC. During her tenure WMC widened its activities and started doing charitable works. They gave educational and marriage aids for poor children's and sisters, support to construct houses, distributing sewing machines, etc. In 1996, Mrs. Leelamma Daniel became the president and during her time many widows were helped, and many poor ladies got financial supports for their marriages. Many women leaders gave leadership to these ministries. When the work got established in different

336 Mariamma Samuel. "Agni Navumai Onnara Patittandukal" One and a Half Decades with fire Tongue: *AG Malayalam District WMC Silver Jubilee Souvenir* (2007): 37-40.

337 Leelamma Daniel, "Malayalam Districtile WMC Pravarthanangal", *South India Assemblies of God Malayalam District Council Souvenir,* 2000, 77.

338 Leelamma Daniel, "Malayalam Districtile WMC Pravarthanangal", 77.

places, local sisters also joined them, travelled around the villages, visited homes and spoke to women, visited orphanages, prisons, etc. In 2005, they founded a shelter home, Snehabhavanam, for the homeless especially for widows and old aged people. At present the council holds a remarkable position in the AG church in Kerala.[339]

## 3.5. Women in the Present Day AG Church in Kerala

There are a number of women in the AG church in Kerala especially in south who are used by God. Some of them are recognised by the Church and others are not. The recognised group are mainly spouse of male leaders. In this section, I will highlight few of them and their contributions in mission field.

### 3.5.1. Annamma Johnson

Annamma is the wife of Late Rev. P. D. Johnson, one of the top national leaders the AG Church in India. He served in different capacities as Superintendent, General Secretary and the presbyter of Thiruvanthapuram section.[340] In 1975 Annamma married P. D. Johnson. Since then God used her to be a strong support to her husband in ministry. She travelled extensively along with her husband throughout India and several other countries. God used them enormously as an evangelists and revival speakers. During that time she was actively involved in the ministry of the church and very mightily being used by God among the women.[341] She had served as the president of the WMC of the Kerala state for several years. God used her significantly and build up women's ministries in different parts of Kerala. Her special interest, commitment and co-operation from many young women and pastors, resulted to a great success and growth of WMC in different churches of Assemblies of God.[342] During this time many women worked hard and prayed constantly

339 An interview with Mariyamma Samuel (WMC President) at AG office, Punalur.

340 A. C. George, *Trail Blazers for God*, 274.

341 Saju Mathew, *Kerala Pentecosthu Charithram*, 252.

342 Interview with Rev. Finny George at Bethel Bible College, Punalur, on 6th March 2015.

for the function of this council. God began to work through these sisters, as a result many miracles occurred through Women's missionary council and it became a lifelong passion for ladies.[343] Many sisters were actively involved in evangelism, visiting homes, and shared gospel. They extended their helping hand by distributing mats and petrol-maxes to the needy and poor, granting sewing machines for the poor and unemployed ladies.

Once Pastor Johnson was invited to Zambia for some revival meetings, after the meeting while he was resting, he was called to his eternal home on 16th October 1990.[344] Annamma helped her husband in various capacities. After the death of her husband, she continued and is still active for the Lord in His vineyard.

### 3.5.2. Mariyamma Samuel

Mariyamma is the wife of Pastor T. J. Samuel (Superintendent of Assemblies of God, South Kerala). She became the president of WMC in 1992. In all these years the council believe that "what people are concerned enough to pray about, they will take action to accomplish." She is a woman of prayer and deeply committed for the mission.[345] As a result of her prayer, and support of her husband, she took initiative to bring changes in the Women's Missionary Council. There are many other servants of God including men and women who sacrificially supported and co-operated in this venture. The social witness of the Women's Missionary Council is praise worthy.[346] WMC extended their service through charitable work, such as financial support for the group of poor ladies in their marriage, financial aids for children, buying property for pioneering work, sponsoring some young men in their theological training,

---

343 Leelamma Daniel, "Malayalam Districtile WMC Pravarthanangal, *Assemblies of God Dhoodhan*, 52/2 (October, 2005): 21. Information collected from Rev. K. S. Samuel at Bethel Bible College.

344 T. J. Samuel, From District Superintendent: *Assemblies of God Doodhan* 52/2 (October, 2005): 2.

345 V. Sunitha Jasmine, *Women's role in Building and Nurturing the Assemblies of God Church in Kerala*, 64.

346 Annamma Johnson, "Missionaries worked in Kerala", *South Indian Women Serve* (Materials collected from AG office).

tailoring, and providing other material for the poor and needy. In the year 2005, they were able to give shelter for the widows and old women, etc.[347]

### 3.5.3. Mary Sam

Mary Sam is another notable woman who served as the secretary of WMC in Trivandrum region and the treasurer for the section CA in Kanjiramkulam. It was through her effort Kanjiramkulam AG church got established.[348] She contributed much towards organising Sunday school, and her ministry was useful for the growth and development of the church. At present there are around 30 church branches added to this Kanjiramkulam church.[349] A significant contribution she made to the Lord's work in this region is adorable.

Apart from the above mentioned women there are others such as Kunjamma Daniel, Marimma George, Shallini Pallickal and Raichel Daniel, etc., who gave leadership to these ministries and actively contributed to the ministry of AG church.[350]

## 3.6. A Brief History of Christianity in Kannur

Kerala or Malayalam is the chief name given to the narrow strip of land which lies between the Western Ghats and the Arabian Sea.[351] Malayalam, another name of the state, which is also the name of the language, is probably derived from mala (hill) and alam (dale) corresponding to the undulating physical feature of Kerala, the land of hills and valleys. And 'Malabar' is a partially arabicized form

---

347 Interview with Mariyamma Samuel, WMC President, at AG Office, Punalur, on 6 March 2015.

348 Sheeba James, *The Ministry of Women in Pauline Writings and its Relevance in the Present Day Churches in Kerala with Special Reference to the Assemblies of God*, 101.

349 L. Sam, *Assemblies of God Doothan*, Vol. 16. No.12 (1970, September 14), 21, Materials and information collected from Mr. L. Sam, Trivandrum, Sheeba James, *The Ministry of Women in Pauline Writings and its Relevance in the Present Day Churches in Kerala with Special Reference to the Assemblies of God,* 101.

350 Leelamma Daniel, "Malayalam Districtile WMC Pravarthanangal", 21.

351 A. M. Mundadan, *History of Christianity in India*, 15.

of the same word. The term Malabar Coast was used by western travellers.[352]

Kannur is also known as Cannanore which is the anglicised form. The meaning of Kannur in Malayalam is 'a beautiful village'. There is also a Sanskrit name for Kannur, i.e., Velapuri which means sea shore town.[353] In some of the ancient literatures one comes across this name. These names and their meanings aptly describe Kannur. It is situated and located in the extreme northern part on the sea shore of Malabar. It is also a beautiful place.[354]

Kannur is in northern side of Kerala, included in the region called Malabar. It lies between Kozhikode (Calicut) and Kasargode districts. Kannur district comes under the Malabar Coast. But later it was known as Malabar District.[355] The Malabar district consists of six administrative district of Kerala and Kannur is one of the districts in Malabar.

Kannur was been known as the popular sea port in the great antiquity. The first Portuguese man Vasco da Gama landed in 1497. It is only around 160 km away from Kozhikode. The primary purpose of Portuguese was business, but later they were also interested in the mission work. This area is economically and educationally backward mainly dominated by Muslims and also has a strong population of Hindus.[356] It also has some tribal belts where people still live in primitive conditions. This was one of the least evangelized areas. As a result of the missionary work of Portuguese many local Hindus and Muslims embraced Christianity.[357] Many of these new converts are from lower caste Hindus. These converts who became Christians were also not faithful ones, as most of them had become Christians

---

352 A. M. Mundadan, *History of Christianity in India*, 15, 17.

353 Jacob Varghese, *Servanthood Evangelism: A Study of the Evangelistic Methods of the AG Church in Kannur District of Kerala,* South Asia Institute of Advanced Christian Studies MTh, 1995 (Unpublished Thesis), 1.

354 Jacob Varghese, *Servanthood Evangelism: A Study of the Evangelistic Methods of the AG Church in Kannur District of Kerala,* 1.

355 Jacob Varghese, *Servanthood Evangelism: A Study of the Evangelistic Methods of the AG Church in Kannur District of Kerala*, 1.

356 A. M. Mundadan, *History of Christianity in India*, 384.

357 Joseph Thekkadath, *History of Christianity in India*, 110.

only for material benefits and to get rid of their low positions. Many Hindu and Muslims girls married Portuguese settlers and became Christians.

Regarding their religious life, Mathias Mundaden says,

> Religious instructions were regularly and systematically imparted to the new Christians and church functions were conducted with all decorum and devotion. Catechism classes were, as a route organized in the afternoons. When vicar rang the bell, all the women and children came to receive the instruction. In 1522 the Bishop of Dune, on a visit to Kannur found everything in order in the fort. He preached there a few times and administrated the sacrament of confirmation to a number of Christians.[358]

The Portuguese had contributed much to Kannur. They had built a good hospital in Kannur in 1505 under the sponsorship of the viceroy Almedia.[359] During those times two churches were constructed inside the fort some time before 1542. In this way the Roman Catholics church was planted in Kannur in the beginning of the sixteenth century itself. They were the pioneers of Christianity in Kannur district of Kerala.[360]

Towards the close of this period a Franciscan monastery was also erected.[361] Though they faced oppositions from authorities, still the missionaries carried out the missions. However, the Franciscans did succeed in baptizing a number of Hindus.[362]

From the sixteenth century onwards many Christian missionaries came and worked in this district. Some of them were Roman Catholic, Anglican, and German. In 1785, the church missionary society established their missionary work in Kannur and started several churches and schools for the education of local

358 A. M. Mundadan, *History of Christianity in India*, 304.

359 A. Sreedharan Menon, *A Survey of Kerala History*, (Kottayam: National Book Stall, 1967), 375-380.

360 A. M. Mundadan, *History of Christianity in India*, 384.

361 A. M. Mundadan, *History of Christianity in India*, 384.

362 Joseph Thekkadath, *History of Christianity in India*, 110-120.

children.[363] There was another missionary organization called Basel Mission. They began their work in north Kerala in the middle of the nineteenth century.

Regarding their pioneering work Godwin Shiri commented in his book,

> The three pioneer missionaries of Basel Missionary society began their journey to India from England on July 12th 1834 and established their mission work in Kannur. In 1839, Dr. Hermon Gundert and his wife arrived in Kannur. He worked zealously for the upliftment of the people in educating and leading them to development. After accomplishing much for mission of God in India, in 1893 he went to be with the Lord. Though, Basel mission did tremendous work in Kannur by uplifting of the poor and needy people, their main ministry was to prepare the field for a spiritual harvest. Others who came after them were benefited by Basel mission's work.[364]

### 3.6.1. Migration of Christians from Central Kerala to the Malabar Area

Most of the Christians in Malabar area are migrated from central part of Kerala and settled down in different places. This migration began in1930s. Since then many Christians came and settled in different parts of Kannur district.[365] The migration of 20th century from south to the north played an important role in the Christianizing of Kannur. Mostly the migrations were to the eastern side, the high land, such as Iritty, Ulikkal, Arabi, and Peravoor. Earlier the Christian population were very less. But after migration the situation got changed and most of the migrants were from Roman Catholics, Jacobites, Marthomites, CSI, Pentecostals, Brethren, Baptists

---

363 Jacob Varghese, *Servanthood Evangelism: A Study of the Evangelistic Methods of the AG Church in Kannur District of Kerala*, 3.

364 Godwin Shri, *Whole in Christ, The Legacy of Basel Mission in India*, (Mangalore: SATHRI Publication, 1985), 340.

365 Jacob Varghese, *Servanthood Evangelism: A Study of the Evangelistic Methods of the AG Church in Kannur District of Kerala*, 4.

and various other denominations.[366] Apart from this many Syrian Christians and few Pentecostals choose to migrate from Travancore (Kerala). A few Roman Catholic churches that were organized by some of the migrated peoples, and some Basel mission churches can be seen in some parts of this district.[367]

The migrated people were hard workers. They came and cleared the hills of jungles and secured very productive land. The Catholic churches were very much interested in the social needs of the people. For that reason they established schools, hospitals, colleges along with churches. The Syrian Jacobite churches also did the same. The land lords of Kannur district were high class Hindus called Namboodiris. They gave away or sold the land to the migrated people.[368]

### 3.6.2. A Brief sketch about the Beginning of Pentecostal Work in Kannur

Some of the Christians who experienced the Pentecostal faith were those who migrated to Kannur area in 1930s and 1940s. During that time this city was the centre of Basel mission. Among the migrated Christians, there were many Pentecostals but they could not find any Pentecostal fellowship due to which many of them joined other Christian denominations. However, as a result of Pentecostal revival in South Kerala, many received vision for Malabar and came to Kannur side.[369]

The earliest Pentecostal work in the Northern parts of the Malabar Coast was started in 1930.[370] Later many were inspired to spread this Pentecostal faith throughout Malabar under the leadership of Pastor K. E. Abraham, Kochukunje Upadeshi, Podimala Mathaichen and K. C. Cherian. It was Pastor K. C. Cherian and V. Thommachen who became instrumental in bringing Pentecostal message in this part of India. Pastor Cherian was one of the early

366 Saju, *Kerala Pentecosthu Charithram*, 235.

367 A. C. George, *Trail Blazers for God*, 59, 63.

368 N. A., "Malabar Suvishesha Pravarthanangalke Oru Pachathalam" [Background of Gospel work in Kannur], *Good News*, (May 1994): 3.

369 Thomas Thannackal, "Kannur Suvisheshi Karanamthinte Pachathalam" [Background of Gospel works in Kannur], *Good News*, (May 1994), 3.

370 Saju, *Kerala Pentecosthu Charithram*, 234.

Pentecostal pioneers in Kannur.[371] During his stay in Kannur he conducted some meetings in Kannathur elementary school near Kannur but without much success in his ministry. Therefore, he left Kannur and moved to Trichur side.[372] P. V. Thomas was another missionary who came to Malabar with his wife as a Pentecostal preacher. He was with pastor Cherian. Later he came to Kannur and worked till his death in 1957.[373]

In 1932, Thomachen came along with his wife Saramma and continued the work over there. They were Pentecostal missionaries. They hired a room in Kannur and began their work. Later Pastor Chirackal Geevarghese also joined them. They conducted many conventions and open air meetings. As a result of these meetings occasionally some people came and attended the worship service to see the mode of worship. Apart from them, there were many other prominent preachers who came to Kannur and conducted special revival meetings but this did not yield any fruit. As a result they had to leave the place.[374]

### 3.6.3. The Early History of Assemblies of God Church in Kannur

In 1932, Miss. C. S. Eddy, a British missionary arrived in Malabar Coast and stayed in Payyampalam in Kannur. She worked very hard to have a church in Kannur. As a result God used her to be an instrument in establishing many Pentecostal churches in northern part of Malabar.[375] Kiriot Paul from Kozhikode helped her in translating message. Later she became an Assemblies of God missionary. In the same year (1932) she opened a mission station in this city and named it "Hebron Mission."[376] By 1934 she was

371 George Daniel, "Malabarile Pravarthanangal Ente oormayil", *SIAG, Malayalam District Council, Souvenir*, 2000, 45-49.

372 Saju, *Kerala Pentecosthu Charithram*, 239.

373 *Saju, Kerala Pentecosthu Charithram*, 239-241.

374 L. Sam, "Assemblies of God Malabar District", *Assemblies of God Doothan* 44/3 (November 1997): 9-11.

375 Archieves Collections from Punalur Assemblies of God Museum.

376 L. Sam, "Assemblies of God Malayalam Districtum Videsha Missionarimarum (Assemblies of God Malayalam District and Western Missionaries)," 99-108.

able to establish a congregation.[377] Her mission was to evangelise the whole Malabar. She was assisted for this task by some faithful native workers. Through her missionary work, many women came forward like Gitty Arnon, and Daisy Michael who were employees of the British Company from Kannur. They got saved and became regular member in her congregation for worship service.[378]Eventually from the East India Company many others also came forward and joined the AG church. During this time a man named E. P. Yesudasan came to Pentecostal faith, and resigned his job and went to Palaghat to start AG work.[379]

With the help of many native workers she was able to start a ministry among the prisoners in the Kannur central Jail. As a result many remarkable things occurred through her ministry. Her involvement in prison ministry gives us a glimpse of the Apostle Paul's ministry to the Philippians jailor. Miss. Eddy narrates that:

The door has opened a door of opportunity for us in the big jail here. Four of the women of the jailors' families have given their hearts to Jesus. One of them was an old woman, and about two weeks after she got saved and the Lord took her home to glory. She was so happy in Jesus and her going home was precious. Two of the others are now hungry for the baptism in the Holy Spirit.[380]

There was another report of the conversion which took place through a miracle healing of a blind woman and a couple. The mission also conducted two Sunday school for the children of that area. They used every opportunity to reach out the unreached. For that purpose they held gospel meetings in the surrounding villages though they had insufficient evangelists and Bible women.[381] Her passion and enthusiasm to train the young people and make use of them for the evangelization of that needy area can be viewed in her statement:

377 C. S. Eddy, "Blessings in South India," 10.

378 Saju, *Kerala Pentecosthu Charithram*, 240.

379 C. S. Eddy, "They want another Religion," *The Pentecostal Evangel* (February 11, 1939), 8-9.

380 C. S. Eddy, "Blessings in South India," 10.

381 A. C. George, *Trail Blazers for God*, 59.

There is one man in our mission who is part of the first fruits of our work here, and he now spend all of his spare time in going out with our evangelist. We are longing to send him to our Bible School in Mavelikara and then take him on as an evangelist here.[382]

Later in 1939, from the Kannur mission, the work was extended to different parts of North Malabar such as Cherikkal, Badagara, Palakkad (Palghat), etc. Later a missionary family Mrs. and Mr. W. E. Davis also associated with her in the mission work in Malabar. She always promoted the nationals, both men and women in the ministry. Her report goes like this:

"I have put an Indian Evangelist and Bible women in Kannur, Cherikkal to care for the work there and an Indian Evangelist at Badagara in charge of that station."[383]

By this time Eddy and her co-workers were able to build up many congregations in that part of Kerala. However, the AG church achieved solidarity and stability, all over the Malayalam areas by the end of the fourth decade of this century.

In accordance with her strong calling, she had to move to Bangalore but she continued to supervise the work in Malabar. In 1939, at the time of the Second World War, according to the government policy, Miss Eddy had to return to her own country leaving the believers of Kannur like orphans.[384] Due to the lack of leadership in the following years the work decayed. Through this great woman of God, the Kannur district had the privilege to hear the gospel. Regarding the AG work in Kannur, an article says, nearly in the year of 1938 Assemblies of God reached in Malabar by David, Miss Eddy and Miss. Escar, and local pastors, Yesudasan, and Wilson. Up to 1948 there was drastic growth in the mission field. Thereafter under the leadership of Pastor K. Varghese, C. E. Mathai, K. A. Varghese, P. J. Samuel and P. T. Chacko, the church established in different places.[385]

---

382 C. S. Eddy, "Blessings in South India," 10.

383 C. S. Eddy, "They want another Religion," 8-9.

384 Saju, *Kerala Pentecosthu Charithram*, 241.

385 P. J. Samuel, "Vellu Viliye Sweekaricha Veeranmar," The Heroes who took the Challenge, *C. A. Silver Jubilee Souvenir, 1931 to 1976*, 102.

In the 1950s Pentecostalism came to the eastern side of Kannur district. The first migrant Pentecostals was Peraparambil Thomas and his family. Gradually there were many other families like Pathalil George and Vithupurakkal Kunjuge who took immersion Baptism. The first Pentecostal worship service was started in Vallithode in 1952.[386] They had no permanent Pastors for some years. Occasionally, some pastors and family used to visit and helped them in conducting worship. Among them were pastor Kukku master from Calicut and Kuttapuzha Kuriachen.[387] In 1956, AG sent a permanent pastor to this church. K. M. Joseph took in charge of this church and served here for some time with his family. This was the first AG church in this part of Kannur district. In later years many new members were added to this church. In the following years many new churches were established in neighbouring areas.[388]

In 1964, Home Missionary Council team of Bethel Bible College came to a place called Kanichiyar. During this period, number of churches was established by the constant missionary effort of HMC. Thereafter every year the HMC team came to Kannur and worked there during summer.[389] In 1968, HMC teams came again for summer ministry under the leadership of Bethel Bible School students. They also conducted some meetings and their initial evangelistic efforts resulted later to pioneer churches in Kannur especially in Malabar. In 1970, they started the first Pentecostal fellowship. The Assemblies of God church played an immense role to sow the seeds of gospel in Kannur District. Pastor V. A. Thomas and his family, T. M. Georgekutty, V. T. Abraham and his wife

---

386 Jacob Varghese, *Servanthood Evangelism: A Study of the Evangelistic Methods of the AG Church in Kannur District of Kerala*, 5.

387 Interview with Pastor J. Selvaraj and wife, at Arabi Church, Information collected from late pastor's wife Mrs. Iype.

388 Jacob Varghese, *Servanthood Evangelism: A Study of the Evangelistic Methods of the AG Church in Kannur District of Kerala, 6.*

389 *Souvenir- Golden Jubilee, Bethel Bible College, 1927- 1977*, Punalur: Assemblies of God, 1977, 17. *Pentecostal Year Book*, (Kottayam: Baruch Printing Press, 1993, 176.

Thakamma, and George Varghese were the initial appointed pastors of these local churches.[390]

During this time, a Pentecostal lady by the name Aleykutty Thavu became a great source of encouragement and support for the Pentecostal ministers in the region. She was one of the first migrants.[391]

The Pentecostal work started progressing in the Kannur district mainly focussing the migrated people located in Iritty, Vallithode, Arabi, etc. These places had main Christian colonies during those times. The earnest prayers, sacrifices and toils of some of the native brothers and sisters resulted immensely in the growth of Pentecostal Churches in Kannur. The Christ Ambassadors and the women's Missionary Council were actively involved in the development of the work.[392]

In 1965, Arabi AG church was established as a branch of Perinkery AG church.[393] Through Arabi church, number of branch churches originated. Many prominent leaders and renounced preachers visited from time to time and strengthened the church. From this church many young people were sent out to the mission field. Arabi church is known as one of the missionary churches in North Kerala.[394] Throughout these years many missionaries including men and women paid a heavy cost for the establishment of churches in North Kerala (Malabar area). We can't forget the valuable service rendered by the women/men ministers in the field of evangelization in Kannur area.

Some of the pastors and their wives who worked tirelessly for the establishment and development of the churches in North Kerala are:

390 Saju, *Kerala Pentecosthu Charithram*, 241.

391 George Daniel, "Malabarile Pravarthanangal Ente Ormayil", 49.

392 Saju, *Kerala Pentecosthu Charithram*, Malabar 1950 nusesham, 240 to 242.

393 Interview with Pastor J. Selvaraj and Family, at their residence, Arabi, January 12, 2015.

394 Jacob Varghese, *Servanthood Evangelism: A Study of the Evangelistic Methods of the AG Church in Kannur District of Kerala*, 11.

### *3.6.3.1. Pastor V. T. Abraham and his wife Thankamma*

Pastor V. T. Abraham is the pastor of the biggest church in Kannur district. He is married to Thankamma, who resigned her job to help her husband in ministry. Their first pioneering experience was at Kannur. As a family both of them worked sacrificially for the growth of this church. As a result they could build up a good Assembly within few years.[395] It should be noted that under their ministry a few co-operative evangelistic bodies were formed, such as 'Love Kannur 93', Decade of Harvest ministries, etc. There are several outreach places started in the district. Thankamma gave a strong support to her husband in all his ministries. Later, they moved to Calicut AG church and continued by pastoring in the church and giving leadership to many other ministries.[396]

### *3.6.3.2. Pastor J. Selvaraj and wife Elizabeth J. Selvaraj*

Elizabeth Selvaraj is the wife of pastor Selvaraj. In response to the call of God, they both came to Malabar and actively involved in evangelistic activities and pastored in different churches. In the year 1980 Pastor Selvaraj was appointed as a full time pastor in the Arabi AG church. From 1980 they have been pastoring this church for more than 35 years. J. Selvaraj and his wife did an amazing work in the surrounding areas of Arabi AG church.[397] God gave them a deeper, more meaning full service in that place. She was a fervent follower of Christ. Her involvement and mission work in that area, including work with the young ladies, inflamed her heart with what became a lifelong passion for leading people to Christ. She showed much interest and commitment to win many souls from that area. Along with her husband, she worked faithfully and tirelessly for all these years. She was a strong inspiration for women folk and prayer warrior for her husband's ministry.[398]

---

395 A. C. George, *Trail Blazers for God*, 272.

396 N. A. "Evare Parijayappeduka (Get aquainted with them)", *Christ Ambassadors*, (Feb-March, 1986): 25, and Jacob Varghese, *Servanthood Evangelism: A Study of the Evangelistic Methods of the AG Church in Kannur District of Kerala*, 10.

397 Interview with Pastor J. Selvaraj, At Arabi church, 11th January 2015.

398 Interview with Mrs. J. Selvaraj, At Arabi church, 11th January 2015.

Regarding their ministry in Arabi, in God's providence ministry grew and expanded. Prayer has been the undergirding that has accompanied them every steps of the ministry ladder one by one. Prayer was so important in her life and her gifts centered praying for others. She longs for others to know her prayer-hearing and prayer answering heavenly father, and she has long sensed the need for woman in the ministry. She gave leadership to Women Missionary Council, and gave opportunities to some able women to lead and conduct women's meetings once in every week either in the church or in any other homes. She conducted prayer cells every day in parsonage.[399] There were good number of ladies who have gathered together with the same burden and passion to intercede for perishing souls. With the co-operation of sisters in the church, they started outdoor ministries as well. Their ministry was focused on visiting homes, distributing tracts, personal evangelism, counselling, open air meeting, pioneering church. All these years sister Elizabeth played an important role in ministry and contributed significantly to the growth of the AG church in Arabi.[400] Over the years she have formed a lot of very strong ties with them and the affection she got from the believers stand in line forever. Those of whom who worked intimately with her valued her prayerful life.

Elizabeth worked hard and prayed constantly in conducting local meetings for the women in Arabi church. Some of the ladies that attended in the meeting become the strongest pillars of the work in that area. Her prayer life motivated other ladies in the church to take part in church activities. She played a key role to invite ladies and encourage them to participate in meeting every once in a week without any fail. Pastor Selvaraj and Elizabeth have given untiring service for the Lords ministry. God enabled both of them to accomplished through preparing many Evangelists and Gospel workers to carry the word of God in to the needy fields.

---

399 Jacob Varghese, *Servanthood Evangelism: A Study of the Evangelistic Methods of the AG Church in Kannur District of Kerala,* 10.

400 Interview with few of the ladies of this church and collected materials from them. The writer herself been the member of this church she is the eye witness for the growth and development of the AG church at Arabi.

During the term of their service in that area, many truth seekers Christians from Roman Catholics, Jacobites even from Marthoma background came out. They themselves opened their hearts to the biblical doctrines from their traditional way of worship. One of the main reasons for this breakthrough was that the people became more acquainted with Pentecostal experiences and many miraculous events occurred. The researcher herself is one of the witnesses of this revival. During the pastoralship of Pastor Selvaraj and family, Arabi AG church grew rapidly. In the years followed, God raised many prayer warrior women along with Elizabeth to give a strong support to this ministry. Some of them are Sister Baby, Sis. Kunjamma, Sis. Mariyamma, and Sis. Thankachi. Their sacrificial labours have enduring results in the great hosts of warriors for the everlasting Kingdom of God. God kept them as strongest pillars of the work in that area and the church. [401]

Even though, Pastor Selvaraj and Elizabeth are physically weak, but the passion and zeal for Jesus is compelling them to be continue in God's service. In spite of these draw backs, God is strengthening them to carry out the ministries. They have been Pastoring the church for the last 35 years. For the past 35 years of their faithful service has been a source of blessings and encouragement for all the believers. Today, more than one hundred members gathered together for Sunday worship.[402]

We could highlight the best example from the Bible, and in the Christian ministry the church has a tremendous challenge to highlight the role models of the Aquila- Priscilla couple, who could work and stay together even when the wife gains priority at times because of her charisma. Therefore, the writer is a firm believer, without question, that behind every successful man is a sensible woman. The opposite also should be true: 'there is a man behind every successful woman'. As men and women, we need to stand together in all aspects of God's mission of transformation and see the kingdom being established mightily.

---

401 Interview with Mrs. Elizabeth Selvaraj at her residence, Jacob Varghese, *Servanthood Evangelism: A Study of the Evangelistic Methods of the AG Church in Kannur District of Kerala*, and Data Collected from believers of Arabi church.

402

When we go through the contribution of women towards the origin and growth of the AG church in Kannur District, there are innumerable unforgotten godly women, missionary wives, religious sisters who have contributed their maximum time, energy, and all resources they had for the sake of gospel. There were women aiming at the salvation for all souls. They worked tirelessly through teaching, prayer, sacrifice or charitable service. There were women prayer warriors, who have been mightily used by God with their limited capacities in different ministries. They were ordinary women-housewives, mothers, teachers and daughters who sacrificed and toil their lives for the Pentecostal faith.

These unnamed brave and devoted women provide to us a vivid picture and story of the significant role that ordinary women have played in the history of the Charismatic and Pentecostal movement. It seems that God in His infinite mercy and wisdom endowed some special gifts and qualities to the women which enabled them to have an attitude of better receptivity and adaptations to show their potential as an achiever.

Even today, there is an immense need for women to take part in reaching the unreached for Christ. More than 50% of those who believe in Christians in India are women. If that 50% of the body of Christ is not involved in mission, the task would be gigantic. When women are enabled to reach other women, ministry becomes exceedingly effective. Therefore, we need to recognize the importance of women's contribution and the unlimited opportunities they have to reach the world with the Gospel of Jesus Christ. God has given women all the gifts of the Spirit and we need to acknowledge it by providing space for the great mission of God to reach all people groups. Women are not only great prayer warriors but also effective counsellors they can empathize well with the suffering ones. Therefore, when they are motivated for soul winning, they can be highly effective.[403]

403 Sakhi Athyal, "Women and men together as God's Agents of transformation", 47.

## Conclusion

There is a proverb 'Having a daughter is like watering a flower in the neighbour's garden." This saying is very much true in the life of women both within the church and outside the church. They are treated as naive and are under the hegemony of the male members of the society. Prejudice against women can be seen very clearly in the church history records and are very much visible in the present church structure. The question needs to be addressed is, could we reinstate the inherent value and the hidden potential of women? Could we do a proactive role to ensure freedom to exercise the potential of women? And could we restore the historically misplaced, unrepresented and isolated women who played a pivotal role in the origin and growth of church?

The male historians contributed immensely to place a record of the origin and growth of the church in Kerala, but a closer scrutiny and research reached to an astonishing conclusion that throughout church history women too in spite of limitation contributed immensely to the church and Society. Unfortunately, the male historians perhaps due to the norm of the culture ignored the role of women who worked with male counterparts behind the growth of the church. The contributions of women go unrecorded.

The researcher in course of investigations found out that there are scores of women both foreign and native who played a central role both in theological training and church related activities. The researcher strongly feels that if women in spite of limitations did maximum in the past, had they given freedom the present position of the church would have been better.

The researcher strongly feels that there is no dearth of theological colleges where women are trained, but implementation parts needs to be relooked with a positive mind frame as women constitute a major proportion in the church. The women and her expertise need to be acknowledged to make the church more vibrant and effective.

Chapter 4

# Leadership Development Programme for Women in Assemblies of God in Kannur District

## Introduction

This chapter contains the analysis of the believers' (men and women) view regarding the subject, 'Leadership development programme for women in the AG church in the Kannur district'. The research work was done in the Kannur district of Kerala among the AG churches. The project was done mainly through empirical study. The researcher has distributed around 150 questionnaires for data collection in the AG church, mainly in Kannur district. The collected data is evaluated by coding and tabulation method. The researcher also conducted personal interviews with few prominent leaders of AG church. These data and personal interviews helped me to analyse the strength and also some drawbacks in the leadership development programme for women. The data also provided some suggestions to empower the status and role for women in the ministry.

## 4.1. Demographic Details of the Respondents

### 4.1.1. Graph One: Age Group

Analysis: The respondents were categorised under six groups. The reason behind is to ascertain the views of different age group. The researcher strongly feels that the view of leadership will differ in each age group. The female teenagers who excelled in academics both in schools and colleges argues that if in secular realm, women can compete with men, why not in church and theological college?

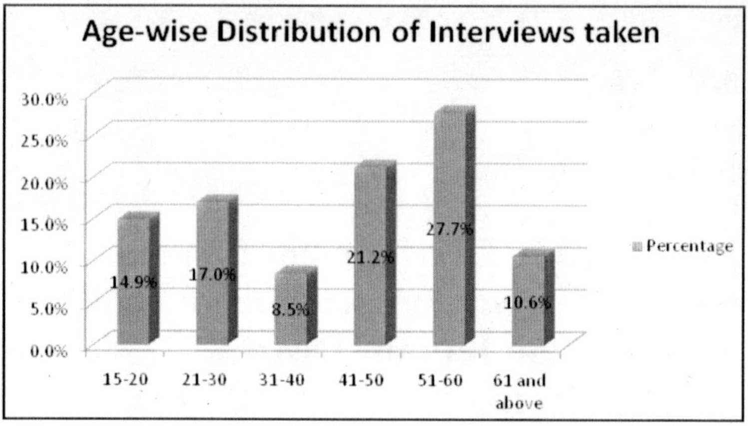


## 4.1.2. Graph Two: Gender

Analysis: The respondents were both male and female. The purpose behind this is to know the feedback of male members regarding

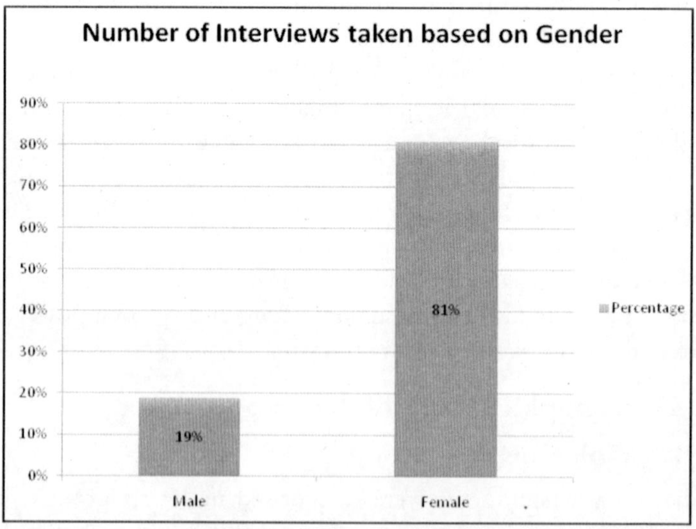

leadership role of women. The views of women were taken to know whether they are willing to accept leadership role in the churches. Often women especially of age group 51-60 and above are passive in approach. They express that for generations we are given subordinate role and it will continue. These views are however, not acceptable by age groups 15-20, 21-30 and 31-40.

### 4.1.3. Graph Three: Marital Status

Analysis: The respondents were both single and married. The rationale behind is to determine whether leadership role given to women will disturb the individual, family and the church. The general observation among the male members is that biological and cultural differences hinder women to leadership role. This view is categorically opposed by the majority of women. They argue and counterattack by referring secular field.

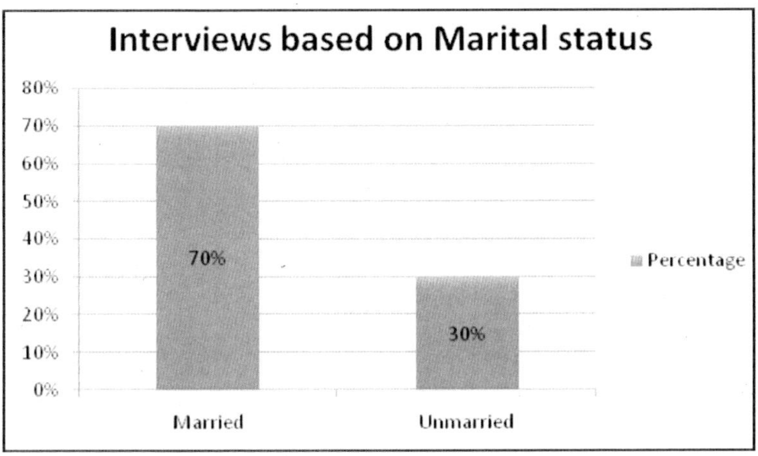


### 4.1.4. Group Four: Position in the Church

Analysis: The respondents position in the church are taken due consideration to agree on the pros and cons of women leadership. There is a general feeling that male members are uncomfortable to accept women as leaders over men. This is true as for years men were at the forefront and women at the backseat. To accept women equally potential to men and to offer leadership role will take time.

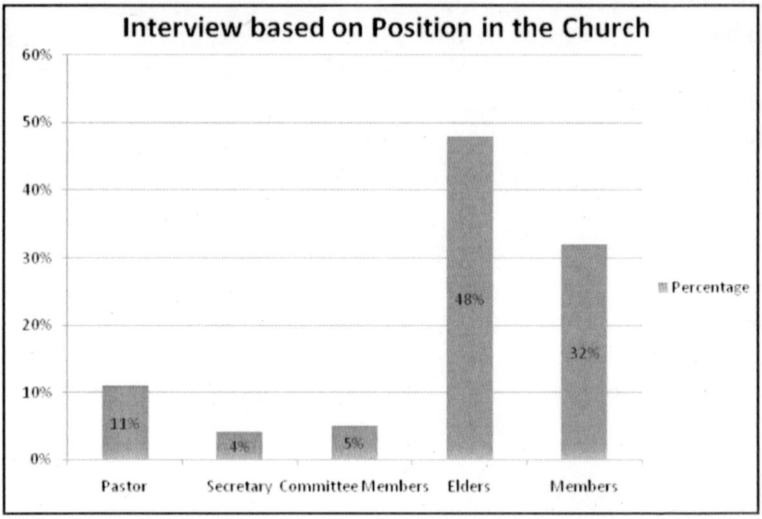


## 4.2. Survey on 'Leadership Role of Women in the Assemblies of God in Kannur'

### 4.2.1. Figure One

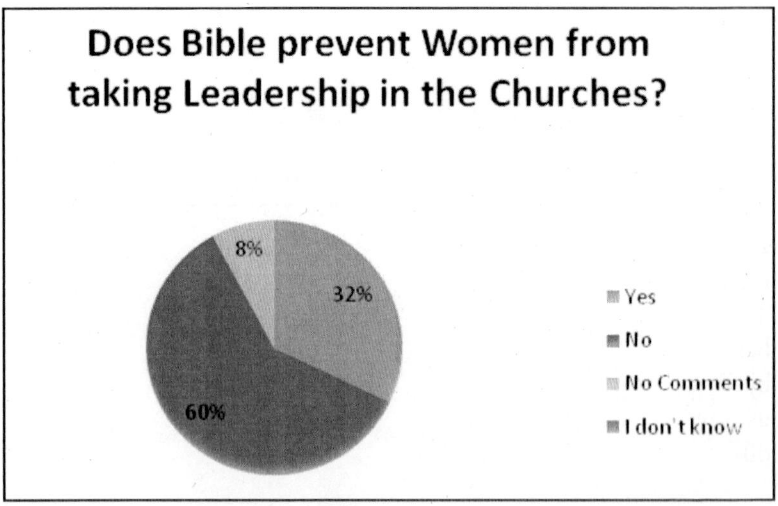

Analysis: It is quite alarming to note that 60% of the respondents feel that Bible does not prevents women from taking leadership in the church, whereas only 32% mainly male respondents argue that Bible doesn't support for women leadership.

Since a majority favours for women leadership based on Bible, the important question needs to be addressed is: If both Bible and believers supports for women leadership, why opportunities are not given to women?

### 4.2.2. Figure Two

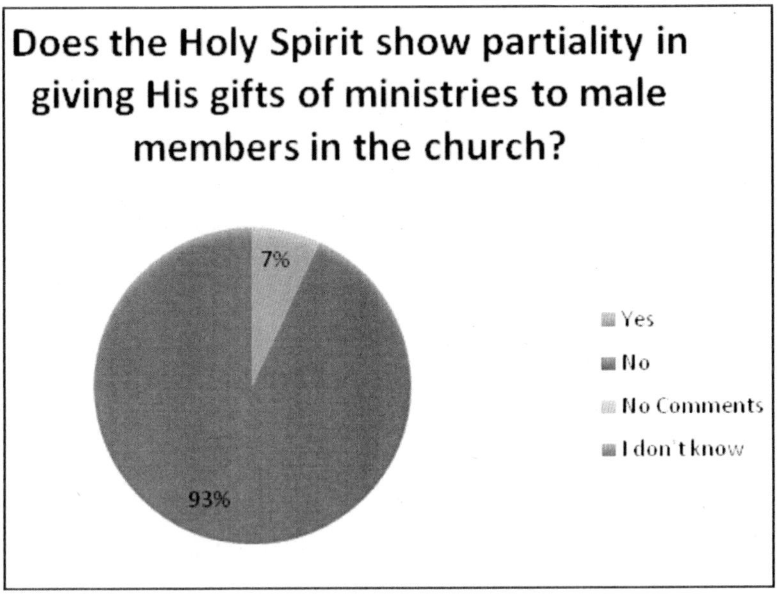


Analysis: Whopping 93% favours the notion that Holy Spirit does not show partiality in giving His gifts of ministries to the male members in the church. A meagre 7% argues against the notion. This figure clearly points out that the gifts of ministries are equally bestowed upon both male and female which is clearly endorsed by Prophet Joel and NT writers. Both the Bible and history gives us ample references where women like men were used by God in different forms of ministry.

## 4.2.3. Figure Three

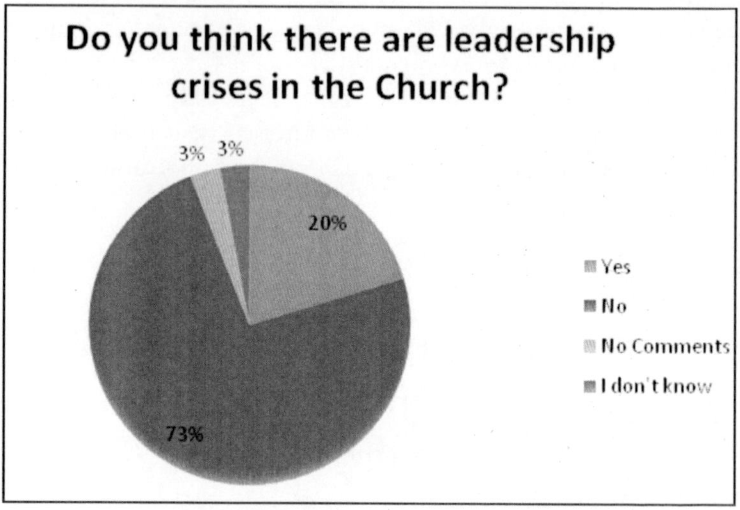


Analysis: 73% respondents strongly feel that there are no leadership crises in the church. However, the leaders are male members of the church. It is high time to sort out this issue. As mentioned, women constitute more than half the congregation. This crisis situation can be sorted out by giving ample opportunities to women leaders.

## 4.2.4. Figure Four

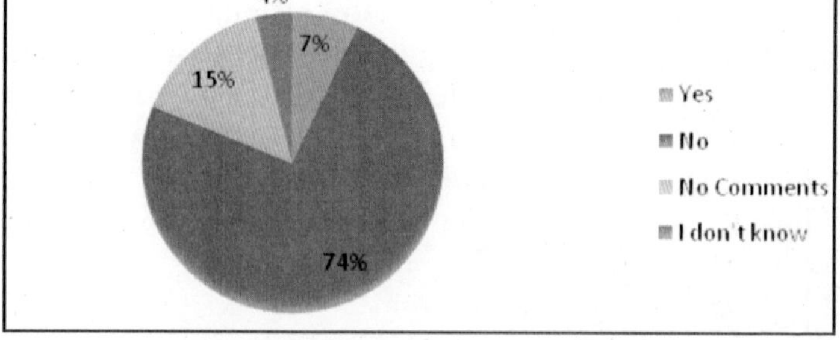

Analysis: 74% respondents are of the opinion that the church allow women's leadership participation in Sunday worship and a tiny group 7% are not in favour of women leadership. The question needs to be addressed is, if majority are in favour to have women as leaders, what is stopping in executing it?

### 4.2.5. Figure Five

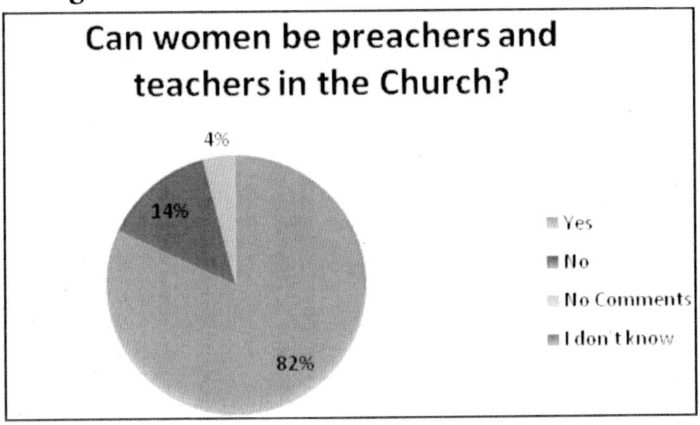


Analysis: 82% respondents are of the view that women can be preachers and teachers in the church. Only 14% disagrees with this view.

### 4.2.6. Figure Six

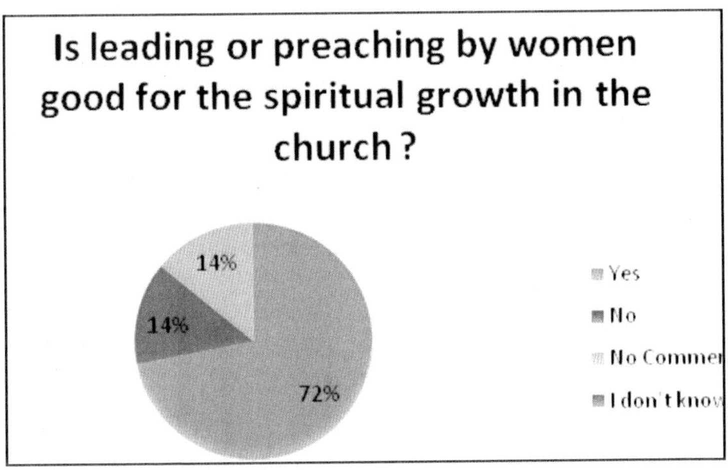

Analysis: Whopping 72% respondents are of the opinion that women as leaders and preachers are good for the spiritual growth in the church. Only 14% feels it negatively.

### 4.2.7. Figure Seven

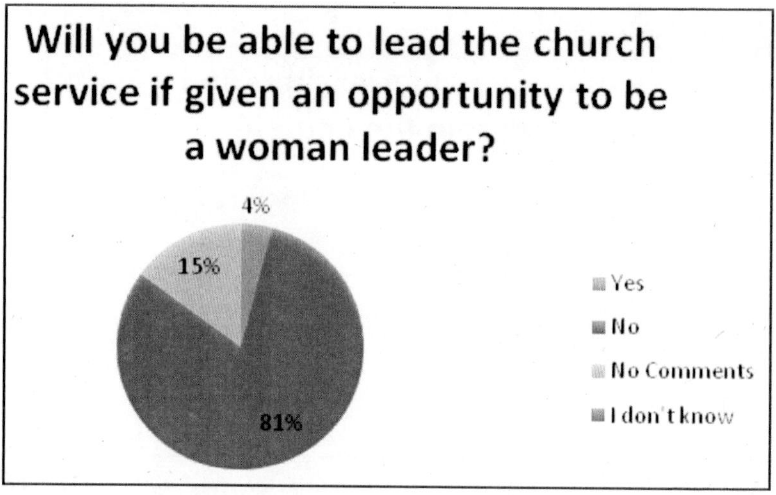


Analysis: It is a discouraging note to say that 81% respondents are not confident enough to lead the church service. The reason behind this is the cultural barrier which is dominant in the church that makes women as passive and dormant.

### 4.2.8. General Evaluation

The researcher has analysed the views of different age group, church goers both male and female, leaders and common people to know their opinion about the present day status and role of women and contribution in the growth of AG church in Kerala. The data collection mainly highlights the intricacies of the issue of women's ministry and leadership in the AG church. The major drawbacks I have found throughout this is that though women constitute the major constituency in the church and are actively involved in spiritual retreats and prayer fellowships, but unfortunately their contributions are taken lightly and often decimated by the male counterparts.

The pertinent question needs to be addressed is: There are many capable women; some are even much more intelligent and capable than men then why they are not recognised in the church?

The researcher strongly feels that some bold initiative is needed to address this crucial issue. The way out is only by providing reasonable space to women both within and outside the church. Formulating Leadership development programme for women and implementing is one of the possibilities to address this pressing need.

## 4.3. Challenges and Prospects

Recognising the contribution of women in the past and promoting women in a higher level in church is one of the important challenges of our day. There are various factors which are responsible for exclusion of women from leadership roles in the church. The main factor that contributes to women's insignificant role is the rigid traditional structures, which needs to be deconstructed. A proper investigation is needed to draw out all other factors behind the exclusion of women. In the first place, it is vital to re-visit the history to ascertain the contribution of women; secondly, it is necessary to look at the roles women can play and contribute to the growth of the church and thirdly, what are some of the areas to be developed to promote women as co-partners in the growth of the AG church.

## 4.4. Critical Study of Women's Leadership Role in the Assemblies of God in Kannur District, Kerala

In the AG church, women's experiences show that instead of an upward movement, there is a backward movement. For example, in the early years of AG churches in Kerala, there were women who pioneered many churches, preachers, and evangelists whose roles were similar to those of men in the same positions. The only major difference during those days was that the men were only ordained and recognised which is not so in the case of women. Though, both male and female contributed almost equally behind the origin and growth of the AG church but the privileges which includes the right to preside over the church activities was solely entrusted to men. In present day, though in secular realm women reached to a promising height, but women in spite of all credentials are not given ample opportunity to prove their leadership skills.

The pioneer Assemblies of God Bible College (Bethel Bible College) was initiated by foreign women missionaries. But the sad reality is that the staff and faculty at present day is hundred percent male. The dream of the founders was to train young men and women to reach the unreached with the gospel, but now the leadership enrols only male students. If a female member is interested, she is expected to attend evening classes or special classes during summer days. The reason for discouraging co-education is unhealthy relationships. If so, why women are non-beneficiary in theological training?

The AG church is almost 150 years old. The researcher interviewed both male and female church leaders. Both male and female leaders in unison agree and recognise the fact that women are contributing immensely behind the growth of the church and are strong pillars of the church but only male members are recognised and credited for this growth. It is interesting to note that the main donors are women working as nurses and pharmacists in States and in other Western countries, who toil hard to build up the kingdom of God but their names and contributions are never acknowledged in public gathering or in electronic media.

While one might expect that the role of women would have increased or at least been persistent over time, in fact, the researcher through interviews found out that whatever roles of ministerial leadership they held earlier are taken away from them. The progress of women in theological education is not in proportion to their appointment to leadership positions in the churches. Today, on the one hand, there is participation of women in the life of the church at the grass-roots level, but on the other hand capable and well-qualified women are excluded from leadership roles except in women's organizations. Even in the women meetings they are not given free hand. The male leaders generally preside the meeting. The position of women is to coordinate the meetings. These women have no voice in determining their roles. In many church bodies they are excluded from the higher levels of leadership where the decision making conversations occur. Moreover, they are denied the privilege of voting in the local church administration. Most women remain involved only at the level of local church ministry, missionary service, or education. This is a general trend in almost all churches and Bible Colleges. As a result they are often been left out of institutional leadership and thus rarely appear in the official documents of denominations.

### 4.4.1. Theological Training

In the early days of the Pentecostal movement in India and especially in Kerala, theological education was not a must for one to enter into the ministry. There was a common feeling that higher theological education was a hindrance to the spirit filled ministry. A number of the native pioneers of the early Pentecostal movement had no or little theological education to their credit, as they believe that their authority to minister did not come from the standards of this world or academic qualifications but by the experience of the Holy Spirit Baptism and the exercise of the gifts. Gradually this misunderstanding changed and male members undergo theological trainings. However, this wrong understanding badly affected the women, as the male members feel that women can do service like prayer and hospitality. For women at the most basic theological training is enough.

Even today there are less theologically trained women in the AG church, Kannur. As a result when the issues of women's involvement in the church and ministry come they are grouped under the category of a weaker and marginalised section/ the subaltern of the society. They are treated as inferior. Consequently, the women themselves prefer to remain passive. I assume that this kind of treatment is meted out not only among the AG church, Kannur but also in almost all churches. This may be one of the possible reasons for the decline of women's active involvement in church activities, and many are occupied and satisfied as housewives. Even those women who are interested to serve the body of Christ and are actively participating in church activities are not encouraged and stamped as part time members. They do not have any form of leadership roles not even as members of committee. They are not given preaching responsibilities even if they are talented than male counterparts. If they come out with those wrong prejudices and minister, the male counterparts find it difficult to acknowledge them in public and in writings, with a very few exceptions. This is the pathetic situation of women in the churches of Assemblies of God. Because the trained women are not given ample opportunity to minister in the church and in Bible Colleges, there seem to be fewer women candidates coming forward for theological training from Kannur. It is therefore very essential to empower women.

The researcher argues that the churches and theological leaders should broaden their mindset by recognising the rights, ability, and intelligence of women counterpart. The women folk too should not underestimate their God given potential. They can come to a new understanding of themselves, who they are and what they can do, what it means to be God's creation in God's image as well as members of Christ's body and that they would no longer bow under male traditional dictation. This awakening may help them to understand their status, role and freedom and full participation in the church and ministry. This awakening is not within women alone rather many men are awakened to this greatest awareness of women's and men's equal status and role.[404]

## 4.5. Leadership Development Programme for Women

It is important to analyse first of all, the factors that are hindering women to actively involve towards church leadership roles and participate fully in mission. Some of them are:

### 4.5.1. Inadequate Leadership Roles given to Women due to Patriarchal Prejudice

The most important aspect is the way in which the church reflects the inflexible patriarchy. This patriarchal domination that continues to uphold male superiority and female inferiority and subordination of women to men hinder women from leadership role even today. No church is free from patriarchy, as the patriarchal structure of the church excludes women from all leadership roles. The women sense uncomfortable with it, even if they cannot walk away from it. The greatest barrier against women is traditional values and practices. It

404 R. L. Hnuni, *Vision for Women in India*, 156.

is essential to break down all these barriers. Unfortunately, in almost all churches still it remains a taboo to appoint women in a position of a leader.

### 4.5.2. Lack of Theological Education/Training and Lack of Women Empowerment/Awareness Programmes

Women are not given ample opportunities to prove their leadership. The fact that many women find it difficult to rise above are because of their low esteem about themselves. This may be another factor which needs to be addressed. It is possible only by empowering them. Because of the underlying ideology prevailing in the male dominated culture, the women cannot become leaders. This is seen mainly in Pentecostal churches and colleges.

In my survey I came across women who are still labelled 'as weak.' These women instead of rising amidst criticism prefer to be passive by accepting that they are incapable and unable to do much in men's world. They find difficult to climb the ladder and overcome the underlying notion that subordinate them. This is perhaps because of the culturally imposed negative label. It has a lasting impact upon women. Even capable women have developed this self-understanding of being weak and that made them, unable to do many things which they could in fact do. The negative tag damage or lessen their potential, marginalise, and make them lose their self-confidence. For this reason women need theological training which can empower and equip them so as to be able to rise up above what they think of themselves. The leaders and teachers in theological colleges should have a brain storming session to address the issue: Why are women trained? Do we train women to limit them to be a minister's wife or part time teachers? The answer to these questions will enable women to take up leadership and prove themselves that they are able. They need to be told constantly that they are capable and they have great gifts and talents that God would like them to multiply and make them channels of blessing.

### 4.5.3. Conventional Interpretation of the Scripture

Some of the educated women (secular& theological) in the AG church plainly expressed during the course of interactions that women's ministry in the church is still not accepted by the male members. This is due to the biased interpretation of the scripture. Hence, the ministries of women are unrecognised. This shows that we need to re-visit the Scripture and have a very heavy task in making women's ministry equally important in the growth and development of the church. In order to do these, the church have to understand the biblical basis for women's ministry?

Unfortunately, there is a misconception that in the Bible women is not included in the ministry. Moreover, whether it is marriage or a common gathering, the male preachers often quote Apostle Paul's letter to substantiate the point that female is subordinate and hence remains silent both in Church and public places. Misquoting and misinterpreting Scriptures, therefore prohibit women from full fledge ministry.

Since, the Bible is a central source of inspiration and norms of life for doing Christian theology, traditional and wrong interpretations of the Bible have been keeping women in loggerheads even in this globalised world. It is true that since the Bible was written by male and from a male-dominated society, the Bible contains androcentric languages and characters which are used as a tool to reinforce patriarchal domination.[405] Hence, they have been interpreted by males to suit their hegemony. The misinterpretation or one-sided interpretation has greatly compressed women's ability and creativity. This is one of the factors that are diminishing the role of women as AG leaders.

Barbara L. Cavaness[406] points out some of the positive steps based on Bible and need of the Church in the far progressive changing world:

---

405 R. L. Hnuni, "Feminist Theology: History, Meaning and Concern", in *Transforming Theology for Empowering Women*, ed. R. L. Hnuni, (Jorhat: Women's Studies, Eastern Theological College, 1999), 172.

406 Barbara. L. Cavaness, "Leadership attitudes and the ministry of single women in Assemblies of God missions" in *Philip's Daughters*, 127-128.

1. Respect for God's call and anointing equally on women as on men
2. Belief that the church was in the "last days;" and needed every willing hand for evangelism
3. Recognition of ministers by the acceptance and ordination of women as evangelists, church planters, missionaries, and many other leadership roles.
4. Reciprocity in sharing of pulpits
5. Appointment of women to leadership positions
6. Recognizing the influence of women in many fellowships.

In reverse order, the "top six" negative leadership attitudes that increasingly restricted ministering women are:

6. Attempting to legislate (through resolutions and publications) the extent of God's call upon women
5. Believing that the "weak shoulders" of women cannot carry the responsibilities of institutions they have started, so strong men should take over
4. Devaluating the efforts of women and using fear of "feminization of the church" in attempts to encourage more men to assume leadership
3. Desiring acceptance among "older and wiser" denominations that restrict women in leadership
2. Believing that letting women lead means bringing all the evils of secular feminism into the church
1. Acknowledging that while "God may choose to use women, we prefer not to, and we really think the Bible says we shouldn't."

The above mentioned 'reverse order' almost resembles with the different views of the male members regarding women's active participation in ministry and their role in leadership development programme in the AG church, Kannur.

## 4.6. Proposals for Empowering Women Leadership in the Church

The main areas in which women can or should be involved in the life of the AG churches are:

1. Women fellowships office bearers at all level should be women.
2. A proportionate activities within the Church and outside should be entrusted to women. Such activities can be carried out by both trained and untrained women in the AG church.
3. As Sunday school teachers and assistants to the heads of Sunday school programmes. If women are capable and theologically trained they can even head the Sunday school.
4. Part of committee members.
5. Exposure programmes.
6. Streaming out potential and talented girls to develop them for leadership including pastoral and higher level leadership including pastoral and superintendent level leadership.

## 4.7. Final Assessment

The above analysis shows that in the AG churches, women continue to play traditional low status roles in the ministry. In the light of my survey, it is alarming to note how the churches are depriving the potential of women which constitute half of the people. It is a high time to pause and ponder whether women are entering into full participation for God's mission or whether they are entering into the 'structures' of the church. After a survey of over scores of churches, it is true that women in this area are lagging way behind and need to be equipped for leadership role in the churches. While a few women in churches are seeking the right to serve, the institutional churches for the most part neither recognise the need for their service nor encourage them in the development of their rights.

Hence, it is at this stage that women are called by God to challenge the traditional structures. They should make determined and intensive effort to change the 'power positions' to 'service opportunities'. They should become the scruples of the church, constantly demand, reshape reviews and revisions until their goals are aligned to the mission of the church in the context they live. Women need to be prepared, and equipped for true stewardship. Today most of the women are habituated to be passive in leadership role. So we also need to think of ways and means for equipping women and to make them come forward to offer their service in church and mission.

Hence, from the above survey, in view of women's alienation due to their exclusion from church roles, it is urgently necessary to challenge and bring the alteration in leadership by equipping women in different ways to take up the responsibility. Even it is an acknowledged fact that the leadership represented by male members in different aspects of life including theological education has not been satisfactory as it is so much patriarchal oriented and male prejudiced accompanied with autocracy. In many mission organisations, Bible colleges and churches the highest leadership responsibilities are still in the hands of men, even though women are almost equal to the number of men in missions and missionary training programs. Through leadership development programme we can expect great impact among women in the future days.

## 4.8. Areas to be Re-looked for a Healthy Body of Christ

1. The uncertain set of rules and regulations that are rigid and closed need to be revised to allow every member the right to participate.
2. Tokenism is to be avoided as it undermines the abilities of women to minister in their own right.
3. There needs to be revision of the prescribed text on Sundays to include women's contribution and leadership as found in the scriptures.
4. There should be women Sundays where women will coordinate all the events.
5. Platform for women's leadership in all gatherings needs to be implemented.

## 4.9. Need for Women Leadership Development Programme

Ever since the coming of Christianity and the establishment of the church in Kerala women played an important role in evangelisation, church planting and in various aspects of Church related activity. They continue to be the limbs of the church in various ways. However, women are excluded from all decision-making bodies especially in the ministry of the church. While the condition of women has considerably improved in all government sectors there is no corresponding improvement as far as their status and position in the church is concerned. Often they are excluded from responsible positions. Since women are the most oppressed, subjugated, the most discriminated, and the most underdeveloped they are the ones who need empowerment and development in all aspects of life.

To empower women means to be in cohesion with them and to be acquainted with the hidden potential and to make use of them. It is not merely confined to powerful words of encouragement, while that is not to be ignored; more important is the practical and implementation aspect of it. This involves their status and role in the church. The way women are labelled and regarded in the family and church as weak, unable, incapable, and inferior, subordinate to men has weakened them much more than they actually are. This type of women's self understanding makes them more vulnerable. Because of this understanding women are not given their due roles and responsibilities in the family and church. Due to this low self esteem women also often refuse to accept the responsibilities which are given to them in the church. Let us look at some of the areas in which women need empowerment in the leadership role of the church.

### 4.9.1. Family

The home-and-family tends to be a forgotten place even though it is a basic instruction within the largest society. However, it is the best place where husband and wife develop into an interpersonal relationship, where patriarchal attitudes, ideas and values are reinforced daily in all aspects of family life. Children grow up with stereotyped roles defined for their lives as male and female. The pattern of relationship between man and women, husband and wife is one of a superior and a subordinate, as perpetuated and accepted by social and cultural conditionings. Therefore, it is important to impart the importance of partnership between husband and wife at the time of giving marriage counselling.

The home, being a most basic social and educational institution, must be transformed. The woman's role and contribution should also consider as an initial step to build up a happy family. Educating the young, especially in the formation of minds and hearts, inculcating new values following the vision of the new order where equality, love, justice, and peace will reign. This is the place where mutual understanding is deeply rooted based on the Christian understanding of God. The need for creating a new form and pattern of relationship between man and woman, husband and wife must be approached on a more personal level. When we speak of empowering women in the family, it is important to have seminars not only in the level of those who have understanding, but also among husbands and wives, so that women empowerment will be more effective. It is necessary however, for the Christian woman to keep a proper balance of activities in her life. Woman should give due priority to her family. On one hand there are cases where women are so busy that they fail to pay proper attention to their husband or to their children. If so, they will not be able to do an effective service for the Lord. On the other hand, some women use their home and families as an excuse for not getting involved at all.

According to Sarah Kovoor, her husband's strong support motivated her into ministry. Her husband was helpful to her in many ways which includes taking care of a number of things in ministry. So we must first get our priorities set and then plan out a balance for serving God, our family and our work and with the help of the Holy Spirit be able to overcome any obstacles to grace and to serve God wholeheartedly.[407]

---

407 Interview with Sarah Kovoor (Daughter of Mary Kovoor, pasturing at AG Pentecostal church in Missouri, USA) at New life Bible College, Cheruvakkal, Kerala, on 17th 2015.

### 4.9.2. Theological Colleges and Christian Organizations

Not only in the family, but also in theological colleges and Christian organizations women have a greater role to play. Women are active and important members; there is no organization where women can't take part. In fact their presence and contributions will bring the organizations to a greater height. Opportunities for theological education for women and recognition of the contribution of women in the field of the theological training have to be given importance. But the sad reality is that right in Kerala there are Bible Colleges initially started by western missionary ladies or single women. The vision behind these colleges was to enrol women to be trained and equipped, but it is very heart-rending to say that today those Bible colleges are being closed down for women. Theological education for girls from the grass root level in both urban and rural areas is important. This will be of great help to the stability of the churches. Male and female partnership at different levels gives steadiness in ministry. It is good to conduct male and female consultation programme concerning women's inclusion in leadership levels. Awareness and realization need to be given in this regard. This is one way of encouraging and empowering women to involve in decision making bodies.

At various international conferences, for example, the role of women is significantly less than that of men. Often, only a token number of women participate in any given international conference. Further, most of the time, men's voices are heard and women keep silent. It goes without saying that this is also the case with regard to positions of leadership at Bible colleges or theological seminaries in the Pentecostal tradition. It seems that we have still a long way to go before women are elected to leadership position in the churches and missionary organizations. Women should be encouraged to take up leadership roles in preparing missionaries and establishing churches.

I would encourage female academicians to join such societies, participate with them, and even organize conferences when the opportunities arise.

### 4.9.3. The Need for a Major Change in the Structure of the Churches

The leadership awareness programmes for inclusion of women in leadership is the present need of the church. Church as the body of Christ consists of men and women created as responsible persons to reach out the unreached. But this truth which is often expressed in writings and accepted in theory but it is too often ignored in practice. Remodelling and restructuring the church is essential.

The shabby treatment meted out to women for years cannot be completely eradicated in a few years. The women should be encouraged to assume leadership responsibilities in the church, in Sunday school, Youth league, etc. This should also be reflected at the higher levels of the church leadership too. Each department of the church committees should involve women. Women can serve as evangelists and missionaries. They can head even organizations, orphanages, and hospitals. These all ministries should become the gate way of the gospel of Christ. If possible, encouragement should be given at the regional and global levels for the upliftment of women.

The women workers' job description is very much important in the growth of the churches. Women workers' training and study centres are essential to improve the condition of women in every place. One of the biggest advantages of having women as partners in ministry is to make deeper relationship with other women which in turn will lead many of them to the Lord. New converts especially women are eager to share their new found faith in Christ with other women.[408]

The limited participation of women in the church's decision making bodies and processes should be abolished. The use of the Biblical text to limit the full participation of women, the undermining of the gifts of women, the use of bigot language in its liturgies and documents, and the old method of marriage ceremony preaching should be abolished.

The importance of mother and father while taking son or daughter to make them to sit in the church during the marriage time,

---

408 Vasantharaj Mano, "Small Beginning to Bring Big Changes", *India Church Growth Quarterly*, 8/1 (April-June, 2001): 10-11.

signing the register by both mother and father should be encouraged. It is quite promising to say that in Kerala many changes have been taking place in this regard, the writer herself is an eye witness to the above event.

### *4.9.3.1. The Multiple Roles that Women Can Play in the Ministry of the Church*

Women too can play multiple roles like Pastoral Care giver, cell group leader, Sunday school superintendent, minister's wife, preacher, Social group, etc. Men and women together in partnership can enhance God's Mission. Above all women can play a big role in the lives of children and youths who are the future of the Church. From the time a baby is conceived to old age, women are instrumental. Many mighty men and women are the results of praying mothers.

The churches must accept the contribution of women and be ready for any kind of changes which is right and good for the well being of the body of Christ. The statistical and survey report presented in this research is helpful for the churches to improve the condition of women. Mass media can be used to remove the prejudices against women. Network of women through inter-faith, inter-denomination, regional and national conferences, and seminars should be held periodically. There is a need to have inter-church discussions time to time on the problems that hinder women from equal participation in the ministry of God. This will help the churches to develop harmony and fellowship in the future church. The churches should come out of the ties of patriarchy and patriarchal structures to challenge the society.[409]

All these attempts would enhance women's entry into the ministry of the church. Each Christian woman needs to have a firm grasp of the world events. God's power is given to women to be used and not to be a dormant. The myth of women being incapable, emotional and irrational must be erased totally. Above all, attitudinal change is very important. This should be brought about only by

---

409 Priscilla Singh, "Women: the Ecumenical Intervension," *To Minister or to Administer? Perspective on Church Administration,* edited by, Jusudas Athyal, Madras, The Accademy of Ecumenical Indian Theology and Church Administration, 1994, 62- **65.**

being receptive to listen to each other, to learn with gracefulness and willingness by both women and men. Since women and men are the partners in the building of the Kingdom of God on this earth, each one is to safeguard the dignity and honour of each other. Therefore, we should allow ourselves to be confronted by the Spirit of God in identifying those aspects of our institutions which are unjust and demeaning and in discovering what changes have to be brought about. The Spirit of God which is poured on all flesh (Joel 2; Acts of the Apostles 2) would accomplish this. As long as there is life, there is hope.

# Conclusion

Let me conclude with the statement of Pamela J. Scalise

> Like men, women who are called by God into Christian ministry cannot escape their responsibility to obey that call. Women who have been blessed by God with gifts, which enable them to serve, are not exempt from service because they are women.[410]

The increasing impact of patriarchal ideals and structures within the church makes women passive resulting into the exclusion of women from leadership roles. For this reason it is essential that women need to have their hold in exercising their God given gifts. They need empowerment and strong support to execute different responsibilities in the church. The more a church is involved in such development programme, the less they are likely to practice patriarchy and I believe such environment can create a deep awareness among women's future and their potential. If they will not get chances or opportunities to learn and develop, there can be no development. When we speak of empowerment of women, verbal encouragement will be of very little help. We need to give them responsibilities and opportunities, and then only empowerment will come to fruition. At the same time, on the part of women too it is important to recognize their God given responsibilities. It is important to develop self-esteem that they are able and can do better. I am of the strong

410 Pamela J. Scalise, "Women in Ministry: Reclaiming our Old Testament," *Review and Expositor*, Vol. LXXXIII, no.1, (1986): 12.

conviction that if women are given enough opportunities, they can greatly contribute to the church and society in greater measures in the years ahead. This is the best foundation of self-empowerment for wholistic leadership role in the church. Women together with men will have to break through traditions and cultural practices that keep them in their respective gender roles. This involves a long and painful process. Women will have to help themselves, first of all, to break out of the roles defined for them, the image and the position that restrict them from creativity and freedom. By working through this at the personal level, both men and women enter consciously in to an equal and mutual partnership in the total life and mission of the church.

It is a well known and well-accepted fact that women are the backbone and limbs of the church. They are the people who form half of the total population both in secular and religious community. Their importance either in the church or mission and ministry cannot be denied while their contributions are highly valued and regarded. Church is the place where women can carry out mission and ministry of the LORD.

In my dissertation research, I come across, notable examples of the commitment of many early female AG missionaries. Among them there were several Spirit filled women, native and foreign missionaries who worked fervently in the forefront and their unique experiences give motivation to many in the Pentecostal faith. It is also true that from the early period, women missionaries fully co-operated with male missionaries and were co-labours in their ministry, yet their role and contribution in the mission field is unrecognized. In fact it surprises me that neither the history of AG nor the Pentecostal historians in Kerala do give adequate record and attention to the extensive contribution and significant roles that women played in the past.

The possible reasons for women being passive are:

1. The church structure right from the beginning are patriarchal and hierarchical where there is no place for women to exhibit their inborn potential.

2. The lopsided theological teachings popularising only selected and controversial passages subjugate women. There was no deliberate attempt to enhance their leadership roles. The cultural norms added to further suppression.
3. Lack of education, opportunities for thinking and acting limited them to their home life.

We can add a lot more reasons for the exclusion of women in the mission and in their writings. But it is more important to learn from the mistakes of the past so that in future they do not recur. Above all, we need to recall the mission of the church and to analyse whether, the church today is an embodiment of that vision.

The leadership development programme for women if implemented properly will enhance the growth of the AG Church.

# Bibliography

## Books


Anderson, Allan., *An Introduction to Pentecostalism*, Cambridge: University Press, 2004.

Athyal, Leelamma, *Man and Woman: Towards a Theology of Partnership*, Thiruvalla: Christava Sathya Samathi, 2005.

Athyal, Sakhi M., *Indian Women in Mission*, Bihar: Mission Educational Books, 1995.

Ayroor, Daniel, *Keralathile Pentecosthu Sabhakal*, (Pentecostal Churches in Kerala), Mavelikara: Beersheba Bible College, 1985.

Bauckham, Richard, *Gospel Women: Studies of the Name Women in the Gospel*, Michigan: Wm B. Eerdmans Publishing Company, 2002.

Beaver, R. Rierce, *American Protestant Women in World Mission*, Grand Rapids, Michigan: Wm. B. Eerdmans Publishing Company, 1980.

Brooten, Bernadette J., "Early Christian Women and their Cultural Context," in *Feminist Perspectives on Biblical Scholarship*, ed. Adela Yarbro Collins, 65-92, Chico, CA: Scholars Press, 1985.

Brooten, Bernadette J., *Women Leaders in the Ancient Synagogue*, Chico, CA: Scholars Press, 1982.

Burgess, Stanley M., *Dictionary of Pentecostal and Charismatic Movements*, ed. Stanley M. Burgess and Gary B. McGee, 118-127, Michigan: Zondervan Publishing House, 1988.

Cartwright, Desmond W., "Your Daughters Shall Prophesy: The Contribution of Women in Early Pentecostalism," Gaithersburg: MD, 1985.

Cook, Robert F., *Half a Century of Divine Leading and 37 Years of Apostolic Achievements in South India*, Tennesse: Church of God, 1955.

Cox, Harvey, *Fire from Heaven: The Rise of Pentecostal Spirituality and the Reshaping of Religion in the Twenty-First Century*, Cambridge: Da Capo Press, 1995.

Cunningham, Loren and David Joel Hamilton, *Why Not Women?* Seattle: YWAM Publishing, 2000.

Damilelon, Jean, *The Ministry of Women in the Early Church*, London: The Failt Press, 1961.

Dayton, D., *Theological Roots of Pentecostalism of Pentecostalism*, Massachusets: Henrickson Publishers, 1987.

Fander, Monica, *Historical-Critical Methods: Searching the Scriptures*, Vol. 1 *A Feminist Introduction,* ed. Elisabeth Schüssler Fiorenza, 28-41, New York: The Crossroad Publishing Company, 1993.

Fiorenza, Elisabeth Schüssler, "Missionaries, Apostles, Co-workers: Romans 16 and the Construction of Women's Early Christian History," in *Feminist Theology: A Reader,* ed. Ann Loades, 70, Great Britain: SPCK 1990.

Fiorenza, Elisabeth Schüssler, *In Memory of Her: A Feminist Theological Reconstruction of Christian Origins*, New York: Crossroad, 1983.

Firth, C. B., *An Introduction to Indian Church History*, Serampore: The Indian Theological Library, 1961.

Flower, Rosewell, *Origin and Development of the Assemblies of God,* Springfield: Gospel Publishing House, 1952.

George, A. C., *Trail Blazers for God: A History of the Assemblies of God of India,* Bangalore: SABC Publications, 2004.

George, K. M., *Christianity in India through the Centuries*, Secunderabad: Authentic Books, 2007.

Gill, Deborah M. and Barbara Cavaness, *God's Women then and Now, Study Guide*, Springfield: Grace and Truth, 2007.

Gryson, Roger, *The Ministry of Women in the Early Church*, trans. by Jean Laporate & Mary Louise Hall, Minnesota: The Liturgical Press, 1976.

Hardesty, Nancy A., *Women Called to Witness: Evangelical Feminism in the 19th Century*, Knoxville: University of Tennessee Press, 1984.

Harkness, Georgia, *A Historical and Theological Inquiry*, Nashville: Abingdon Press, 1972.

Hnuni, R. L., "Feminist Theology: History, Meaning and Concern," in *Transforming Theology for Empowering Women*, ed. R. L. Hnuni, 9-15, Jorhat: Women's Studies, Eastern Theological College, 1999.

Hnuni, R. L., *Vision for Women in India*, Bangalore: Asian Trading Corporation, 2009.

Hoell, Nils Bloch., *The Pentecostal Movement: Its Origin, Development and Distinctive Character*, London: George Allen & Unwin Ltd., 1964.

Hosier, Helen Kooiman, *100 Christian Women who Changed the 20th Century*, Secunderabad: OM Books International, 2000.

Hurley, James B., *Man and Woman in Biblical Perspective*, Grand Rapids: Zondervan Publishing House, 2001.

Jasmine, V. Sunitha, *Women's Role in Building and Nurturing the Assemblies of God Church in Kerala*, Delhi: ISPCK, 2013.

Jeyaraj, Daniel, "The History of Christianity in India: An overview from a Protestant Perspective" in *Missiology for the 21st Century: South Asian Perspectives*, ed. Roger Hedlund and Bhakiaraj, 195-211, Delhi: ISPCK, 2004.

Johnson, T. G., "Munpe nadannavar, Munpil nayichavar", *Halleluah, Pentecostal Year Book*, ed. Samkutty Chacko Nilambur, 193-276, Thiruvalla: Plensy Sam Publisher, 2015.

Kafer, Donna, *Women of Courage*, Orlando: Bridge-Logos, 2007.

Kydd, Ronald A. N., *Charismatic Gifts in the Early Church*, Massachusetts: Hendrickson Publishers, 1984.

MacHaffie, Barbara J., *Her Story: Women in Christian Tradition*, Philadelphia: Fortress Press, 1986.

Massey, James, 'Holy Spirit Led Mission in North India' in *Missiology for the 21st Century: South Asian Perspectives*, ed. Roger E. Hedlund and Paul Joshua Bhakiaraj, 251-259, Delhi: ISPCK, 2004.

Maxwell, L. E., *Women in Ministry*, England: Victor Books, 1987.

McGee, G. B. and S. M. Burges, 'India' in *The New International Dictionary of Pentecostal Charismatic Movements*, ed. Stanly Burgess, 118-127, Grand Rapids, Michigan: Zondervan Publishing House, 2001.

Menon, A. Sreedharan, *A Survey of Kerala History*, Kottayam: National Book Stall, 1967.

Menzeies, William.W., *Anointed to Serve: The Story of the Assemblies of God,* Missouri: Gospel Publishing House, 1971.

Mundadan, A. M., *History of Christianity in India*, Vol. 1, Bangalore: CHAI, 1989.

Powers, Janet Everts, "Pentecostalism 101: Your Daughters Shall Prophecy", in *Philip's Daughters: Women in Pentecostal-Charismatic Leadership*, ed. Estrelda Alexander and Amos Yong, 133-151, Oregon: Pickwick Publications, 2009.

Ruether, Rosemary and Eleanor Mclaughlin, (eds.), *Women of Spirit: Female Leadership in the Jewish and Christian Traditions*, New York: Simon and Schuster, 1979.

Ryrie, Charles Caldwell, *The Role of Women in the Church*, Chicago: Moody Press, 1970.

Saju, *Kerala Penthacosthu Charithram*, Kottayam: Good News Publications, 1994.

Sam, L., "Assemblies of God Malayalam Districtum Videsha Missionarimarum (Assemblies of God Malayalam District and Western missionaries)," *Aathmaniravinte Nooru Varsham: A History of Assemblies of God in Kerala*, edited by Finny George, 99-108, Published by AGMDC, 2015.

Samuel, T. J., "Keralathil Pravarthicha Videsha Missionarimar: A.G. Missionarimar", *Halleluah: Pentecostal Yearbook,* ed. Samkutty

Chacko Nilambur, 277-280, Thiruvalla: Plensy Sam Publisher, 2015.

Shri, Godwin, *Whole in Christ, The Legacy of Basel Mission in India*, Bangalore: SATHRI Publication, 1985.

Stanley, Susie C., "Wesleyan/Holiness and Pentecostal Women Preachers: Pentecost as the Pattern for Primitivism," in *Philip's Daughters,* ed. Estrelda Alexander and Amos Yong, 19-37, Oregon: Pickwick Publications, 2009.

Stephen, M., *New Trends in Christian Theology*, New Delhi: Serial Publications, 2009.

Stephen, M., *Towards a Pentecostal Theology and Ethics*, Kottayam: Chraisthava Bodhi, 1999.

Thekkadath, Joseph., *History of Christianity in India*, Bangalore: Theological Publication in India, 1982.

Thomas, V. V., *Dalit Pentecostalism: Spirituality of the Empowered Poor*, Bangalore: Asian Trading Corporation, 2008.

Torjesen, Karen Jo., "Reconstruction of Women's Early Christian History," in *Searching the Scriptures*, ed. Elisabeth Schussler Fiorenza, New York: Crossroad Publishing Company, 1993.

Trask, Thomas E., "Ask the Superintendent", Enrichment, Spring, 1997.

Tucker, Ruth A. and Walter L. Liefield, *Daughters of the Church: Women and Ministry from NT Times to the Present,* Grand Rapids: Zondervan Publishing House, 1984.

Tucker, Ruth A., *From Jerusalem to Irian Jaya*, Grand Rapids, MI: Zondervan Publishing House, 1983.

Virginia, M. M, Febella, Park, Sun Ai Lee (ed), "We dare to Dream, Doing Theology as Asian Women," New York: Orbis Books, 1989.

Warner, W. E., "Women, Role of," *The New International Dictionary of Pentecostal and Charismatic Movements*, ed., Stanley M. Burgess, Zondervan: Library of Congress Cataloguing-in-Publication Data, 2002.

Woodbridge, John D., *Great Leaders of the Christian Church*, Chicago: Moody Press, 1988.

Yong, Amos., *Discerning the Spirit(s): A Pentecostal-Charismatic Contribution to Christian Theology of Religions*, Sheffield: Sheffield Academic Press, 2000.

**Journals and Souvenirs**

Abraham, T. Valson, "Trumpet: Faith of our fathers", *IPC Platinum Jubilee Edition*, 9, 1, (1991): 1-24.

Athyal, Sakhi, "Women and Men together as God's Agents of Transformation", *Journal of Theological Education and Mission,* 5, (2014): 35-47.

Athyal, Sakhi, "Transformation of Ministry Partnership Vision: Women and men Together as God's Agents of Transformation", *Journal of Theological Education and Mission*, 5, (2014): 35-47.

Bass, Dorothy C., "Women's Studies and Biblical Studies: A Historical Perspective," *JSOT*, (1982): 6-12.

Burgess, John H., "Bible School Proves Blessing", *Pentecostal Evangel,* (May 18, 1935): 6.

Burgess, Stanly M., "Pentecostalism in India: An Overview" *AJPS* 4/1 (2001): 85-98.

Cavaness, Barbara, "God Calling: Women in Assemblies of God Missions", *Pneuma,: The Journal of the Society for Pentecostal Studies,* 16, 1, (1994): 49-61.

Daniel, George, "Malabarile Pravarthanangal Ente oormayil", *SIAG, Malayalam District Council, Souvenir*, (2000): 49.

Daniel, Leelamma, "Malayalam Districtile WMC Pravarthanangal", *South India Assemblies of God Malayalam District Council Souvenir,* (2000): 77-78.

Daniel, Leelamma, "Malayalam Districtile WMC Pravarthanangal, *Assemblies of God Dhoodhan*, 52/2 (October, 2005): 21.

Daniel, Leelamma, "Malayalam Districtile WMC Pravarthanangal", *AG Doodhan*, 16, 12 (September, 1970): 77-78.

Daniel, Raichel, "Nammude Missionarimar, Malayalam Districtle WMC Pravarthanangal", *SIAG, Malayalam District Council, Souvenir*, (2000): 39.

Daniel, Raichel, "Nammude Missionarimar", *Assemblies of God Doodhan*, 52/2 (October, 2005): 37.

Duplessis, David, "Pentecost", *A Quarterly Review of World-wide Pentecost Activity*, 30, (December, 1954): 17.

Eddy, C. S., "They want another Religion," *The Pentecostal Evangel* (February 11, 1939): 8-9.

Eddy, C. S., "Blessings in South India," *The Pentecostal Evangel* (September 22, 1934): 4.

Fiorenza, Elisabeth Schüssler, "Feminist Theology and New Testament Interpretation," *JSOT*, 22(1982): 32-46.

Fountain, A. Kay, "Where the spirit of the Lord is...' *Dharma Deepika*, (January-June, 2005): 33-40.

George, A. C., "Pentecostal Beginnings in Travancore, South India", *AJPS* 4/2 (2001): 215-237.

George, Finny, "AG Yile Chila Adhyakala Pravarthakar", *SIAG, Souvenir*, (2000): 57.

George, Finny, "Keralathile Assemblies of Godnte Ulbhavaum Valarchayum" (The origin and Growth of Assemblies of God) *Doothan*, (February, 1995): 8.

George, Finny, "Karthavil Niriyatheyaya Mrs. Aleyamma Kunjummen", *Assemblies of God Doothan* 41/12 (August, 1995): 16.

Ginn and Graner, "God's Noble Vine" *Golden Jubilee Souvenir*, Bethel Bible College, (1927): 7.

Ginn, Mildred and Lydia Graner, "Students on Evangelistic Tour", *World Challenge*, (October, 1957): 7.

Graner, Lydia H. and Mildred C. Ginn, "Another forward step" *Pentecostal Evangel*, (March 4, 1951): 12.

Graves, Carl F., "Encouraging News from South India", *Pentecostal Evangel*, (February, 1933): 9.

Guthrie, Stan., "A Woman's Place in Missions", (Global report), World Pulse, (April, 2000), 306-314.

Hedlund, Roger E., "Nationalism and the Indian Pentecostal Church of God", in *Indian Church History Review*, Vol. XXXII, (June, 1998): 91-103.

John, Santosh, "Feminism: A Contemporary Theological Critique", *Conviction: Journal of Bethel Bible College*, 1.2 (2013): 56-63.

Johnson, Annamma, AG and the women workers, *SIAG, Malayalam District Council, Souvenir*, A publication of the Malayalam District Council (February 29, 2000): 82-84.

Kowalski, Rosemarie Daher, "The Mission Theology of Early Pentecost: Call, Challenge, and Opportunity", *Journal of Pentecostal Theology*, 19, 2 (2010): 265-291.

Kucera, Martha, "Bible School proves Blessing", *Pentecostal Evangel*, (May 18, 1935): 13.

Kucera, Martha M., "Report", *The Pentecostal Evangel*, (August 19, 1933): 4.

Kunjummen, Aleyamma, "Report," Assemblies of God Bethel Bible College Golden Jubilee Souvenir, 1927-1977: 13.

Kunjummen, C., "The Early History", *Bethel Bible School Golden Jubilee Souvenir*, Punalur: Bethel School, (1977): 4-5.

Kurian, V. Mathew, "Syrian Christian and the Political Economy of Kerala", Indian Church History Review, XXVIII, (June 1994): 89-104.

Mano, Vasantharaj, "Small Beginning to Bring Big Changes", *India Church Growth Quarterly*, 8/1 (April-June, 2001): 10-11.

Mathew, Issac V., "Theological Education in the Malayalam District of A.G.," in *SIAG Malayalam District Council Souvenir* (2000): 53-55.

Mathew, K. J., "Women in Church and Society", Conviction, *Journal of Bethel Bible College*, 1.2 (2013): 17-29.

McGee, Gary B., "Latter Rain" Falling in the East: Early-Twentieth-Century Pentecostalism in India and The Debate over Speaking in Tongues" in *Church History: Studies in Christianity and Culture*, 68/3 (1999): 648-662.

McGee, Gary B., "Baptism of the Holy Ghost & Fire!: The Mission Legacy of Minnie F. Abrams", *Missiology: Tools of the Trade,* XXVII, 1, (1999): 515-521.

Menzies, William W., "The reformed roots of Pentecostalism", *AJPS* 9.2 (2006): 262-282.

Mondal, Geeta, "Women as Change agents in Indian Society", *Dharama Deepika*, (June, 2005): 65-74.

N.a., "New work blessed in South India", *Pentecostal Evangel*, (August 12, 1933): 11.

N.a., "Agni Navumai Onnara Patittandukal" One and a Half Decades with fire Tongue: *AG Malayalam District WMC Silver Jubilee Souvenir* (2007): 37-40.

N.a., "Kunjamma- Saramma Sahodarimar" (Kunjamma- Saramma Sisters), *Assemblies of God Women's Missionary Council Souvenir* (1983): 42-43.

N.a., "Evare Parijayappeduka (Get aquainted with them)", *Christ Ambassadors*, (February-March, 1986): 25.

N.a., "Malabar Suvishesha Pravarthanangalke Oru Pachathalam", (Background of Gospel work in Kannur), *Good News*, (May 1994): 3.

N.a., "Report," *Pentecostal Evangel*, (July 21, 1926): 3.

Pulikottil, Paulson, "As East and West Met in God's Own Country: Encounter of Western Pentecostalism with Native Pentecostalism in Kerala", in *AJPS*, 5/1 (2002): 1-12.

Sam, L., "AG Charithra Rekhal", *SIAG, Souvenir*, (2000): 23.

Sam, L., "Assemblies of God Annum Munpathiel" (Assemblies of God is always in the fore front), *Assemblies of God Messenger*, 41, 6, (1955): 14.

Sam, L., "Keralakarayile AG Missionarymarekurichu Oru Anusmaranam", *Assemblies of God Malayalam District CA Golden Jubilee Souvenir* (2001): 23.

Sam, L., *A.G. Charithra Rekhakal*, SIAG Malayalam District Council Souvenir, 21-23.

Sam, L., "Miss Hodge & Miss Essler- Two Missionary Ladies", *Assemblies of God Doothan* 48/10 (June, 2002): 19.

Sam, L., "Pr. C. Manasseh Thekkan Thiruvtamkurile Adyathe Penthakosthu Susrushakan," Pr. C. Manasseh the first Pentecost Minister of South Travancore, *Assemblies of God Doothan* 40/1 (September, 1983): 5-7.

Sam, L., "Assemblies of God Malabar District", *Assemblies of God Doothan* 44/3 (November, 1997): 9-11.

Samuel, P. J., "Vellu Viliye Sweekaricha Veeranmar", The Heroes who took the Challenge, *C. A. Silver Jubilee Souvenir, 1931 to 1976*, 102.

Samuel, Simon, "The Charismatic and Pentecostal Movements and their Commitments to the Social Demands of the Gospel," *Doon Theological Journal*, 9.2 (2012): 214-246.

Samuel, T. J., "The Origin and growth of Assemblies of God church in Kerala," in *Assemblies of God Doodhan*, (1995): 8-9.

Samuel, T. J., From District Superintendent: *Assemblies of God Doodhan* 52/2 (October, 2005): 8-11.

Samuelkutty, K. S. (ed.), "Assemblies of God in South Travancore", *Assemblies of God Doothan* 48/9 (May, 2002): 17.

Samuelkutty, K. S. (ed.), "The Missionary Lady Who Preached in Malayalam in the Capital City," *Assemblies of God Doothan* 49/ 1 (September, 2002): 11

Scalise, Pamela J., "Women in Ministry: Reclaiming our Old Testament," *Review and Expositor*, Vol, LXXXIII, no.1, (1986): 7-13.

Suguna, Anula Irvin, "The Role of Women in Evangelization", *Kristu Jyoti: A Youth Pastoral Theological Catechetical Journal*, 28, 1 (2012): 12-28.

Tasie, Godwin, "History of Mission: Role of Women in Mission," *Missiology* 7, (1979): 94.

Thampy, Mariamma, "Women and Prophecy: Role of women in This Ministry", *Revive* 7/2 (January-February, 2014): 13-14.

Thannackal, Thomas, "Kannur Suvisheshi karanamthinte Pachathalam", (Background of Gospel works in Kannur), *Good News*, (May, 1994): 3.

Thomas, V. V., "Contribution of Women to the Indian Church: A Perspective from the Pentecostal Churches in India", *SATHRI Journal of Contextual Theology*, 4.2 (2010): 168-184.

William Menzies, 'The reformed roots of Pentecostalism,' *AJPS* 9.2 (2006): 282.

Zacharia, P. N., "Assemblies of God Sabhakal: Arambhavum Valarchayum Ente Ormayil," *SIAG, Souvenir*, (2000): 63.

## Interviews and Unpublished Works

Interview with Mrs. Mariyamma Samuel, wife of Pastor T. J. Samuel, (Superintendent, AG Church), President of the Women Missionary Council, at SIAC, office, Punalur, on 5th January, 2015.

Interview with Pastor Finny George at Bethel Bible College, Punalur on 5th January, 2015, and Archives Collections from Punalur Assemblies of God Museum.

Interview with Pastor J. Selvaraj and his wife at Arabi Church on 18th December, 2014 and information collected from late pastor's wife Mrs. Iype.

Interview with Dr. Issac V. Mathew, Counselor.

Interview with Sarah Kovoor (Daughter of Mary Kovoor, pasturing at AG Pentecostal church in Missouri, USA) at New life Bible College, Cheruvakkal, Kerala, on 17th May, 2015.

Archives Collections from Punalur Assemblies of God Museum.

Assemblies of God *Prarambhanethruthrayam*, An interview with Dr. Y. Jayaraj (about early prominent pastors: Rev. A. C. Samuel, Pastor K. M. Paniker, Rev. C. Kunjummen) by Mulavana Mohan Das.

Das, J. Yesunatha "A Dalit Tribute to Robert F. Cook: The Pentecostal Pioneer in India," (Unpublished Work).

Earl and Arlene Stubbs, *The Assemblies of God in South India*, (Unpublished paper), 1974.

Guthrie, Stan. "A woman's place in Missions", (Global report).

Information collected from Simon Samuel, principal of NTC, Dehradun, on 30th July, 2015, at NTC, Dehradun.

James, Sheeba *The Ministry of Women in Pauline Writings and its Relevance in the Present Day Churches in Kerala with Special Reference to the Assemblies of God*, (unpublished MTh thesis), (Bethel Bible College, 2008), 92-93.

Johnson, Annamma "Missionaries worked in Kerala", *South Indian Women Serve* (Materials collected from AG office).

Karunanidhi, P. "The Situation of Women in the Early Period", History of Christianity.

Missionaries worked in Kerala, South Indian Women serve (Archives collection from Punalur AG).

Oommen, George "Robert Cook: His role in shaping the beginnings of Pentecostalism in Kerala (Unpublished paper presented at the Faculty Seminar on 15th July, 2013).

Skariah, Mathew P. *An Evaluation of the Assemblies of God Church in Kerala and Proposals for the Unity among the Pentecostal Church in Kerala*, 1996, (unpublished thesis), submitted for the degree of Master in theology (FFRC, Kottayam, 1996).

Thomas, V. V. "Contribution of Ziegenbalg and William Carey to India: Challenges to Mission of the Church in India Today: A Pentecostal Perspective (Unpublished paper presented at the seminar on 7th February, 2006).

Varghese, Jacob. *Servanthood Evangelism: A Study of the Evangelistic Methods of the AG Church in Kannur District of Kerala,* South Asia Institute of Advanced Christian Studies MTh, 1995 (unpublished Thesis).

Yesukristhuvinte Eliya Dassan: Autobiography of Pastor K. E. Abraham.

# Questionnaire

I am a student of Senate of Serampore College doing my doctoral studies (D.Min) in the department of Christian Ministry. I am undertaking a research as a part of my academic requirement on the *involvement of women leadership in the Assemblies of God Church.* Kindly help me by answering the following questions. Question may be answered by putting tick (√) against your response or by short answers wherever necessary. All the information that you provide with respect to this study will be kept strictly confidential.

Thank you

**Clara M. Shiju**

Interview Scheduled on:..........................

**Demographic Details**

1. Gender

   ☐ Male ☐ Female

2. Name of the place where you live in

   ☐ City ☐ Town ☐ Village

3. Age

   ☐ 15-20 ☐ 21-30 ☐ 31-40 ☐ 41-50

   ☐ 51-60 ☐ 61years and above

4. Marital Status

☐ Marries ☐ Unmarried

5. Position in the family

☐ Father ☐ Mother ☐ Son ☐ Daughter

☐ Son-in-law ☐ Daughter-in-law

6. Position in the Church

☐ Pastor ☐ Secretary ☐ Committee member

☐ Elder ☐ Member

7. Highest Educational Qualification

   a. Secular......................

   b. Theological.....................

8. Do you know of any women leaders (Past or Present) in your Church?

☐ Yes ☐ No

9. Do you think that Church can grow only by men in leadership?

☐ Yes ☐ No

10. What is your opinion on 'women leadership' in the Church?

..............................................................................

..............................................................................

..............................................................................

..............................................................................

..............................................................................

..............................................................................

..............................................................................

11. Women are in leading positions in communities, in politics, in medical field, etc. Why not women be permitted to take leadership in Churches?

 ..............................................................................

 ..............................................................................

 ..............................................................................

 ..............................................................................

 ..............................................................................

 ..............................................................................

12. Do you think that Bible prevents women from taking leadership in the Churches?

 ☐ Yes ☐ No

13. Do you think that the Holy Spirit shows partiality in giving His gifts of ministries to male members in the Church?

 ☐ Yes ☐ No

14. If your answer is 'no', why then we cannot consider women in leadership positions in the Church?

 ..............................................................................

 ..............................................................................

 ..............................................................................

 ..............................................................................

15. What kind of leadership roles do you envisage for women in the Church?

 ..............................................................................

 ..............................................................................

 ..............................................................................

 ..............................................................................

16. What is your opinion on women as pastors in Churches?

........................................................................................

........................................................................................

........................................................................................

........................................................................................

17. If you do not wish to have women as pastors in your Church, why do you think so?

........................................................................................

........................................................................................

........................................................................................

........................................................................................

18. What are people's expectations from women members in general and women leaders in particular in your Church?

........................................................................................

........................................................................................

........................................................................................

........................................................................................

19. Do you think there are leadership crisis at the Church?

    ☐ Yes ☐ No

20. If yes, how do you describe such crises?

........................................................................................

........................................................................................

........................................................................................

........................................................................................

........................................................................................

21. What are some of the issues involved in the women leadership Crisis?

 ..........................................................................................

 ..........................................................................................

 ..........................................................................................

 ..........................................................................................

22. In your opinion, what are the causes responsible for women's leadership issues?

 ..........................................................................................

 ..........................................................................................

 ..........................................................................................

 ..........................................................................................

23. Does your Church allow women's leadership participation in Sunday worship?

 ☐ Yes ☐ No

24. Mostly what role women can play on Sunday worship? *You can tick more than one*

 (a) Leading Praise and Worship ☐

 (b) Special Song Presentation ☐

 (c) Collecting Offering ☐

 (d) Giving Testimony ☐

 (e) Exhortation ☐

 (f) Assisting in Lord's Supper ☐

 (g) Preaching ☐

 (h) Any other........................

25. In your opinion, can women be preachers and teachers in the Church?

☐ Yes ☐ No

26. Do you think their leading or preaching is good for you to enrich your spiritual growth?

☐ Yes ☐ No

27. If you are given an opportunity as a woman leader to lead the service, will you be able to do it? (*Applicable only to sisters*)

☐ Yes ☐ No

28. If you are asked to suggest any changes in the worship order/ service of your Church, what would be your suggestion?

..........................................................................

..........................................................................

..........................................................................

..........................................................................

29. In your opinion in what way your Church can give opportunity for women leaders to evolve a programme for wholistic ministry?

..........................................................................

..........................................................................

..........................................................................

..........................................................................

30. In your opinion regarding leadership development programme for women, what are the emerging trends among the young generation in your local Church?

..........................................................................

..........................................................................

..........................................................................

..........................................................................

# Index of Subjects

# Index of Authors and Leaders